MODERNIST PARADISE

MODERNIST PARADISE

Niemeyer House | Boyd Collection

text by **Michael Webb**

principal photography by **Tim Street-Porter**

RIZZOLI
NEW YORK

VISIONARY DESIGN FOR LIVING

Modernism was born as a visceral reaction to the fakery and clutter of late nineteenth-century arts, architecture, and fashion. The reform movement, which began in England and rapidly spread worldwide, had many agendas. National romanticism, aestheticism with an oriental cast, a paring away of the inessential, and a return to medieval ideals were among the varied manifestations. The movement's leaders were rational and romantic, seeking to bring good design to a broad public but emphasizing handcraftsmanship, which limited products to an affluent few.

Progressives and reactionaries engaged in a battle that continues to this day. At the Great Exposition of 1851 in London, decorative kitsch and the newest machines were juxtaposed beneath the soaring iron-and-glass shell of the Crystal Palace, one of the world's first prefabricated buildings. The English establishment scorned it; the German public was reportedly enchanted. Steel-frame construction and the elevator liberated the architects of Chicago to scrape the skies, but engineers were far ahead of their peers in creating stripped-down train sheds and bridges, not to mention the Eiffel Tower. Some of these daring structures provoked angry protests from self-appointed guardians of taste, but today they are cherished as historic monuments.

"A great epoch has begun! There exists a new spirit... We claim in the name of the steamship, of the airplane, and of the motor-car, the right to health, logic, daring, harmony, perfection."
— LE CORBUSIER

The impulse to change the world exploded in the first three decades of the twentieth century. Modernism revolutionized the arts and sciences, starting in Vienna and Berlin, leaping across Europe to Moscow and Paris, eventually subsiding on the shores of Britain and North America. It drew on the latest technologies, and was propelled by the idealism of a new century and the trauma of the First World War, which destroyed or discredited the old order. Modernism took root in progressive Nordic countries, struggled for recognition in France and Britain, was tolerated then banned by the Soviets, and became a symbol of progress for the Italian fascists. The roll call of those formative years still dazzles: Picasso and Malevich in art, Le Corbusier and Mies van der Rohe in architecture, Gerrit Rietveld and Marcel Breuer in furniture, the collaborative ventures of De Stijl in Holland and the Bauhaus in Germany, to name only a few of the most famous.

"The New Architecture throws open its walls like curtains to admit a plenitude of fresh air, daylight, and sunshine."
— WALTER GROPIUS

For the Germans, Dutch, and Scandinavians, modernism was more about utility than aesthetics. Their buildings and interiors were utopian in spirit and frugal in execution. Social Democratic authorities and trade unions sponsored public housing, schools, clinics and community centers that were healthy, affordable, and convenient. The housing estates of Berlin have survived eighty years of hard use, a harsh climate and long-deferred maintenance, have been restored, and now attract the great-grandchildren of their first tenants.

"Nothing could shake our certainties, creative calm, or joy of working toward building and expressing our epoch."
— CHARLOTTE PERRIAND

The Weissenhofsiedlung in Stuttgart, a demonstration housing project of 1927 now restored to pristine condition, exhales the springtime freshness of early modernism. So do the recreations of Le Corbusier's 1925 Pavilion de l'Esprit Nouveau and Mies's 1929 Barcelona Pavilion. Familiar from old black-and-white photographs, the experience they offer is as thrilling today as when they were built. In the 1920s, a few enlightened members of the bourgeoisie commissioned modern villas, allowing architects to explore the ideas they yearned to employ on a larger scale. The Tugendhats in Brno, Czechoslovakia, and the Savoye family in Poissy, near Paris, briefly enjoyed their modernist paradises before they were forced to flee. The exodus of creative talent from Nazi oppression scattered the seeds of modernism around the world.

Until it became a haven for European exiles in the 1940s, America stood apart from this ferment of activity and competing ideologies. As Secretary of Commerce, Herbert Hoover declined France's invitation to the United States to participate in the 1925 Exposition des Arts Décoratifs. He believed they had nothing impressive to show, and he was partly right. Even though skyscrapers and grain silos dazzled modernists as much as Ford's production lines, American residential architecture and decorative arts seemed timid and provincial to most Europeans.

Southern California was beginning to stir by the mid-20s. Charles and Henry Greene had pioneered open plans, natural cross ventilation, and outdoor sleeping porches in their luxurious California bungalows as early as 1900. A decade later, Irving Gill employed thin planes of concrete in a slimmed-down reinterpretation of the California Missions, and, in the early '20s, Frank Lloyd Wright strove to create a new American architecture using textured concrete blocks that were poured and tied together on site.

"I found what I had hoped for, a people who were more 'mentally footloose' than those elsewhere, who did not mind deviating opinions."
— RICHARD NEUTRA

Wright's massive houses were inspired by Mayan temples; two of his protégés shifted the emphasis to openness and lightness. Rudolph Schindler was inspired by pioneer modernists Otto Wagner and Adolf Loos in his native Vienna. He came to America to work for Wright in 1917, and launched his career in 1922 with a double house-studio that is still one of the most radical residences in L.A. His compatriot Richard Neutra, who had worked with Erich Mendelsohn in Berlin, followed the same course. These two Austrians were the Apollo and Dionysus of Southern California architecture. Neutra played serene variations on a few basic themes, creating models for the postwar Case Study House program and most mainstream modern houses down to the present. Schindler's raw, edgy experiments laid the groundwork for Frank Gehry and the L.A. avant garde. Both exploited the benign climate of their adopted land, integrating outdoor rooms, patios, and roof decks with their airy interiors.

Elsewhere in the U.S., modernism had a tough time winning acceptance. Most people perceived it as an alien phenomenon, created by foreigners whose politics were as suspect as their morals. In 1932 Philip Johnson and Henry-Russell Hitchcock identified a predominant strain of modernism, christened it International Style, and promoted it in a Museum of Modern Art exhibition that toured to department stores all over America. At the nadir of the Great Depression, people were curious about this brave new world, but the curators stripped away the ideological and social underpinnings of modernism, and presented it in purely formal terms: white walls, flat roofs, ribbon windows, and open plans. Buckminster Fuller's Dymaxion house excited wonder but no buyers; likewise the "House of Tomorrow" experiments that were sponsored by industry and world fairs.

Very few Americans were willing to live that way until modernism had been smoothed out and repackaged in the aftermath of war. Even then, progress was slow. In Southern California, only twenty-five Case Study houses were built in seventeen years, and most of these were middlebrow solutions for the middle classes. The Eames's house studio, constructed from off-the-shelf materials, and the steel houses of Pierre Koenig were truly innovative, but Schindler and John Lautner were considered too radical even for this enlightened program. For every one of these one-offs, ten thousand Americans bought a tract house in suburbia. Prefabrication was a bright idea that only spec builders embraced, and then dressed up in a traditional style. In 1945 thousands ordered Fuller's Dymaxion house, which was to be mass produced in a factory that had made bombers; at the last minute, the designer realized he needed more time to perfect this revolutionary dwelling and only two prototypes were realized.

"We mean to wage war on ugliness, and ugliness can be combated only with what is intrinsically good...'good' because at once seemly and practical."
— MAX BILL

Modernism has lost most of its battles in the U.S. residential market but has won the larger struggle to offer a rational option at every price point. Utopia is, by definition, unattainable to achieve. Houses driven by theory or technology are hard to live in. But daring proposals have inspired pragmatic solutions with broad appeal. Many Americans indulge in or covet obscene excess, but a growing minority appreciates the advantages of spaces as practical and spare as the cars they drive and the clothes they wear. They are discovering the material and emotional benefits of living simply, in harmony with nature, and they are fighting back. Uninformed design committees impose a dull conformity in suburbs and gated communities, while builders rarely venture beyond pale copies of traditional styles. Lawsuits are fought over colors, the height of fences, and the pitch of roofs. But skilled architects and determined owners can evade these tiresome restrictions, and interiors are nobody's business but one's own.

"A piece of furniture is architecture at a smaller scale—or a painting in three dimensions. The goal was to take a concept and mass produce it."
— CHARLES EAMES

Even tract builders have adopted open plans, cross ventilation and indoor-outdoor living—as featured in the progressive bungalows of a century ago, and the 1950s Case Study houses. Good ideas filter down, but it can take a while. The furniture of Charles and Ray Eames, Arne Jacobsen, and the prewar masters were originally intended for the masses but priced for the few. Now decent copies of the classics and inventive work by younger designers are widely affordable. Innovative architects of the 1920s designed furniture as "equipment" for their buildings, since no appropriate alternative was then available. Now there is a wide choice, and living with good design may encourage more people to abandon the tired clichés of "Mediterranean" and "Colonial" exterior decoration, and focus on important issues. Modernism is a means to an end. As energy conservation becomes a more pressing issue, and the price of power soars, mega-mansions and their suburban spawn may become as unfashionable as the Hummer.
— M.W.

Michael Webb **MODERNIST PARADISE**

We cannot relive the past, though many try to do so, immuring themselves
in cramped period cottages and ersatz Georgian mansions, as though the world still
moved at the pace of a horse and buggy. Michael and Gabrielle Boyd are romantics
of a different breed: they embrace the dream of technological and aesthetic progress
that flourished through the first two thirds of the twentieth century. Impassioned
collectors, their heroes are giants of modernism: Oscar Niemeyer, who designed their
house; Roberto Burle Marx, who inspired the landscaping; Gerrit Rietveld, Marcel
Breuer, Jean Prouvé, Arne Jacobsen, and other form-givers, whose furnishings they
revere and use. The Boyds have created a modernist paradise in a setting of great
natural beauty, fulfilling the vision of pioneers in Vienna and Berlin, Paris and Los Angeles.
Those enlightened designers believed that spare, luminous, free-flowing spaces,
rationally equipped with sturdy, portable furniture would enrich the quality of their
owners' lives.

The Boyds' house is located on a secluded street in Santa
Monica. Moreton Bay fig trees form a dense green tunnel with roots that extend like
tentacles along the edge of the sidewalk. They dwarf the eclectic mix of Monterey,
Tudor, and Mediterranean-style houses, and there is little to draw attention until you
come to a row of bottleneck palms, lined up in front of a white brick wall. Immediately,
you sense you've arrived somewhere out of the ordinary.

Open the painted steel gate and you step into a hybrid of south-
ern California and Brazil. Palisades of bamboo to either side suggest that the jungle
is pressing in. Sinuous paths of broken travertine frame palms, their sensuous curves
playing off the rectilinear house. The low wing of bedrooms to the right of the entry is
concealed behind an extension of the white brick wall, with shadows of trees and a
pergola playing across its surface. A lofty, glass-walled living area is set at right angles
to the bedrooms, its facade screened with vertical milled aluminum louvers that complement the projecting roof beams. Through an open front door you can look straight
through the house and across Santa Monica Canyon to mountains that, on a misty day,
evoke those in back of Rio de Janeiro. When the sun is high and a breeze blows in
from the ocean half a mile away, this is an idyllic place to be.

Oscar Niemeyer, the first great master of Brazilian modernism—
who is still active in his hundredth year—sketched this house in 1964 for Joseph and
Anne Strick. He is a maverick filmmaker, now living in Paris, whose talents as a writer,

producer, and director have yielded adaptations of literary work by James Joyce and Jean Genet, a docudrama on urban life (*The Savage Eye*), and an Oscar-winning documentary short on the massacre at My Lai during the Vietnam War. By 1963 the couple and their three small children had outgrown a tiny house by Gregory Ain, a protégé of Richard Neutra, and they bought this spectacular lot with the intention of commissioning a new house from a major architect. Joseph Strick flew to Brazil for the Mar del Plata film festival, and stayed on to explore Niemeyer's buildings. He was dazzled by the curvaceous forms of the architect's house above Rio and the fresh minted monuments in the new capital, and knew he had found his ideal architect.

As a young man, Niemeyer headed a group of innovative architects who, with advice from Le Corbusier, created the Ministry of Education in Rio, the first great monument of Brazilian modernism. His personal language of sensuous shapes and free-flowing spaces infused the Brazilian Pavilion at the 1939 New York World's Fair, and his church and dance pavilion for Pampulha, a new lakefront district of Belo Horizonte in the Minas Gerais region of Brazil. He dominated the international team of architects that designed the United Nations Headquarters in New York in 1947, and he capped these achievements as the architect of Brasilia. He was also a committed member of the Brazilian communist party, who would be driven into exile in Paris after the military coup of 1964, and he had been denied an American visa.

This provoked Strick to send him an eloquent request. "I was shocked and embarrassed that you were not allowed to supervise construction of the United Nations building, and I would like you to design a house for me," he wrote. Though fully extended on his masterwork, Niemeyer agreed to undertake the task on a site he would never see for a client he would never meet, to be realized by a local architect who was unknown to him. (Le Corbusier had undertaken a similar commission in 1948 for Pedro Domingo Curutchet, a doctor in La Plata, Argentina, but he was able to specify the renowned architect Amancio Williams as supervisor).

Strick sent Niemeyer aerial photos of the site, topographical plans, soil tests, and information on his family's needs. Four months later, he received a model and sketches for a house that hugged the edge of the canyon. A free-form roof canopy extended out from the living areas, and the bedrooms were tucked into the bluff below. The goal was to give both levels sweeping views over the canyon, and to free as much of the site as possible for the garden. The parti is an expanded and angular version of the curvilinear Casa das Canoas, which Niemeyer built for himself in 1953. Though the original materials have been lost, a nine-page report in the September 1964 issue of *Arts + Architecture* magazine reproduces the model and the architect's sketches for the first, second, and final designs.

"We present a study in frustration, the defeat of a fine, imaginative design by paralyzing building regulations and their dogged, immovable enforcers," is the opening salvo in a text (probably written by editor John Entenza from information supplied by Strick). Local authorities had refused to allow the subterranean bedrooms on the absurd grounds that they might be sublet and thus lower the tone of the neighborhood, but a savvy project architect could probably have negotiated a compromise. However, the first scheme, so far from being "a fine, imaginative design," seems pinched and schematic, lacking the flow and expressiveness of Niemeyer's own house. Living areas and garage are strung out along the west side of the site, and four narrow bedrooms, bathrooms, and a study are lined up, motel-style, at the lower level. The canopy shades an area beside a pool and children's playroom, but has no organic relationship to the building below.

Pushing the living and sleeping areas to the edge of the canyon was a bold move. "For a film director, waking to this view was much more dramatic than looking at it over a pool," says Strick. However, his wife was less enthusiastic, realizing that—in contrast to the Rio house—there was no high vantage point from which to admire the canopy, and that the two-level plan would be a problem with small children. Niemeyer sent a second, two-story scheme in which an upper-level living-dining room is set back from the edge of the canyon as a transverse bar with a butterfly roof, and the bedrooms occupy the first floor. The service areas and garage project forward and the canopy is gone.

"At that point, I felt I'd given the architect free rein and should tell him what I wanted," says Anne Strick. She recalls sketching a T-plan, in which all the rooms were on ground level, with a lofty living area crossing the site. The sleeping areas would be ranged along the east side, with the master suite overlooking the canyon and the children's bedrooms extending towards the street. To impart a sense of movement to the interior, she asked that the living room be extra high, walled in glass, and stepped down from the kitchen.

This all made perfect sense, but one would have expected Niemeyer, who was working on far grander projects and refused to accept a fee for this small job, to tell his clients to design the house themselves. As an ardent Marxist he had no compulsion to build middle-class family houses in the U.S., and most of the few he built in Brazil were done for himself or friends. And yet, with a tone of polite exasperation, the architect acknowledged the sketch and suggestions, and sent a third scheme. It's more conventional than the first, but much more fluid and practical; "simple and constructive, economical and beautiful," as Niemeyer himself described his final design. If you didn't know who designed it, you might guess that this was the last of the Case Study houses.

Sadly, Joseph Strick never got to enjoy his dream house, for he and his wife split up on the eve of construction. The plans were drawn by a commercial architect, Ulrich Plaut, with remarkable fidelity to the sketches, and he drew on his experience in large-scale building to install steel posts and beams to support the 68-foot-long kitchen-living room. Wood beams that extend across the flat roof were substituted for the concrete that Niemeyer had specified and the sketch suggests that they were intended to project out much further than they do and shade the full-height windows, though it's curious that the projection appears to be greater on the north than the south side. The interiors were supervised by Amir Farr, who had been associated with Neutra.

For Anne Strick, the house "worked stunningly well for the children and for me it was as close to paradise as I ever expect to get on earth." Her eldest son, Jeremy Strick, is now director of the Los Angeles Museum of Contemporary Art, and his earliest memories were of the model and the construction site. The new house had nearly six times the floor area of the Ain. "My mother told me that some of the neighbors weren't well pleased, but visitors to the house were generally delighted," he recalls. "As they stepped into the great living room, the glass framing the canyon,

there was an audible intake of breath." No surprises there; most people fear or hate the unfamiliar at first glance, but after spending a little time with it they are often won over, as happens every day with art at MOCA.

The property was put up for sale in 2001 with no mention of Niemeyer, stayed on the market for two years, and was finally bought as a tear-down by a developer who intended to replace it with a Tuscan mega-mansion. Local architects who remembered the story in *Arts + Architecture*, rallied in its defense, the Santa Monica Landmarks Commission blocked demolition, and a realtor alerted the Boyds. They had recently moved to Santa Barbara but were back in New York to conclude the sale of their Paul Rudolph house. Immediately, they flew out to see the property but Michael's first reaction was "no, we can't go through all this again. The garden had been leveled and there was a lot of deferred maintenance on the house."

Gabrielle pushed hard: "It was perfect for us because it was in run-down original condition, allowing us to rescue many elements that most people would have ripped out. Also, the rarity—it's the only Niemeyer house in North America. If we passed on this one, there would never be another." The question of authorship was decisive. "I had to be sure it was designed by him or I wouldn't have bought it," says Michael. "I'm not going to put all my passion and two years of effort into an anonymous design. Restoring a chair is easy and I'll tackle anything that looks interesting, but a house is unique and demands all your resources. Niemeyer is at the top of my list of modern architects. I adore the sculptural forms, his interaction with Corb, and the decades of superb work."

Michael conceived every detail of the restoration, with assistance from Nigel Briand, an architect who worked on the Rudolph house and shares the view that one should do this kind of work invisibly. The structure was basically sound, and they had to make only a few changes to correct errors in the realization of Niemeyer's detailed sketches. The brick wall that divides the children's bedrooms from the entry path was cut back a few feet from the glass facade of the living room to open up a tiny courtyard that is now densely planted. The city required a two-car garage so this was extended forward of the existing garage to provide archival storage and a new roof deck. Cars are parked in the forecourt in the usual Southern California fashion. Eric Lahmers, who has restored Neutra, Schindler, and Lautner houses, spent three months relaminating the roof, filling and splicing beams where the ends had rotted.

Adding vertical aluminum louvers to screen the front windows provoked opposition from the Landmarks Commission, which argued that they were inappropriate. Lahmers found vintage louvers, similar to those that the architect had used on buildings in Brazil and that Neutra had used in rebuilding his own house in the Silver Lake district of L.A. the previous year. Museum curators, historians and other experts testified that Niemeyer would certainly have specified such a *brise soleil* if he had been on site; whereupon the Commission shifted its ground and argued that they were too authentic and thus diverged from Department of Interior restoration guidelines, which mandate a clear distinction between old and new. The issue was resolved, the manually operated louvers provide the necessary privacy and shade, and the house has been designated as a landmark.

In the 14-foot-high living room, Boyd and Briand stripped out the bookshelves and window benches on both sides, and cut down the tall coat closet inside the door that blocked the flow of space, adding a ledge of travertine like the top of a Florence Knoll table. This echoes the line of the low walls beneath the windows. Existing floor coverings of linoleum and shag rug were recovered with palm wood to add a feeling of the tropics and provide a sense of continuity. The room over the garage had been crudely split in two to provide rental units (exactly what the city thought it had blocked in rejecting the first scheme). The dividing wall was removed and the floor cut away to accommodate an open, unrailed staircase that leads down to a book-lined library, and up to a reading room leading out to a terrace over the new archive-garage.

  The guiding principle was not to replace anything that didn't have to be replaced, and to use vintage materials and fittings wherever possible. The roughcast ceiling was stripped of gold paint, and its recessed lights were supplemented by a branching Serge Mouille chandelier. Suspended cabinets in the kitchen were stained a dark brown. The original pink terrazzo in the master bathroom was refurbished and a vintage straw cloth with a salmon pink backing was applied to the walls. Pink Crane toilet fittings, of a design specified by Neutra and other Case Study House architects, were found in a salvage yard and the room now has true period flavor. Door handles, cabinet knobs, and light switches throughout the interior are original or precisely matched. "Most of the changes were cosmetic," says Gabrielle, who took one of the children's bedrooms to serve as her office. "Some of the finishes had deteriorated and needed to be freshened, but, with exception of the library addition, we did not remodel the house, we restored it."

  For the Boyds, the restoration (which extended over two and a half years) was the culmination of a journey that began in the Bay Area where they married and started to raise their sons, and continued on through Manhattan and Santa Barbara. Each stop posed fresh opportunities and challenges, but the big leap came with the purchase of Paul Rudolph's town house on Beekman Place, one of the most prestigious streets in Manhattan. The architect reserved the triplex penthouse for himself, and leased the three duplexes below, until his death in 2000. The Boyds, who had enjoyed spectacular success in the music business, took the entire house for their collection, and restored the triplex as their home.

  Looking back, the couple see this as an educational experience they are unlikely to repeat. "Rudolph was a genius who went off the rails after 1970," Michael asserts. "The triplex was kaleidoscopic; a laboratory created by and for a very complex and conflicted guy. It spiraled in every direction, and it had thirty-seven levels, vertiginous stairs and galleries, which was just too complicated. We lived there two years, and I never figured it out." They realized they were looking for calm, tranquil, uninterrupted spaces to frame their lives and art, and this was the polar opposite: an assertive piece of constructivist sculpture. Paola Antonelli, curator of architecture and design at MoMA, called it "a beautiful nightmare."

  In reaction to Rudolph's overpowering aerie, they moved to a shady retreat in Santa Barbara; a quiet 1965 steel and glass house by Thornton Ladd that was all dark wood and moss-green marble. Originally described as the "House for a Writer," it was quintessentially American—an ideal setting for the work of Nelson and the Eameses. However, the architecture failed to inspire them, and the town felt too much of a pendulum swing away from the frantic pace of Manhattan. So they

moved for the sixth and—they fervently hope—the last time. "This house is a comfortable fit; instead of telling its own story, it allows us to make ours," says Michael. "The scale and proportions are right, and there's a masterly interplay of volumes. Also, it was designed for a family, not an eccentric bachelor."

The biggest challenge was to develop appropriate landscaping from bare ground, and thus create a dialogue between house and garden. The source for this was obvious, for the Boyds were passionately attracted to the work of Roberto Burle Marx, the Brazilian landscape designer who was Niemeyer's closest collaborator until his death in 1994 at age eighty-four. They worked together on the 1939 Brazilian Pavilion, the Rio Ministry, and many later buildings. Burle Marx embraced and amplified Niemeyer's exuberant forms, extending them into the natural landscape. A passionate collector of rare species with a genius for arrangement, he had a tropical sensibility and created green architecture of great originality and beauty.

Niemeyer may have suggested a landscape in the spirit of Burle Marx to the Stricks, though there is no evidence of this in the surviving sketches. But it's easy to imagine that Farr had seen photographs of Brasilia and the public park and mosaic promenades that the Brazilian master had designed for the Rio waterfront. Biomorphic curves were all the rage in America in the 1950s, and they were a natural complement to the orthogonal architecture. Undulating concrete paths and borders of Mexican blue river pebbles were installed in the front yard, though Anne Strick lacked the resources to elaborate on these.

To restore this hardscape, the Boyds excavated tree roots, repaired the broken concrete, and clad it with a mosaic of broken travertine. To the rear of the house, they raised the circular travertine patio and cut away the concrete steps that lead down to the pool. The garden is set at an angle to the rim of the canyon and the abutment was rebuilt in concrete to replace rotting railroad ties. The steep slope below was stepped and terraced to create a secret garden overlooking the fairway of the Riviera golf course, with stools cut from the trunk of a fallen palm tree. In this context, the sand traps evoke the forms of an Arp sculpture.

For the plantings, Michael relied on his research into Burle Marx's favorite species, and his intuitive sense of what would work together. These included Raffeus palms, ferns, Brazilian ironwoods, and philodendron for the shaded areas along the blue slate driveway, and a mix of five different palms, spiky vellozias, and aloe bainsii in the south-facing entry area. Elsewhere in the front yard are fan palms and lady palms, screens of lacy bamboo, black bamboo, and giant bamboo, black mondo grass, miniature horsetail, and clustering blue fescue. Planters on the Paulupe master bedroom deck contain red-flowering Christ's Thorn and *Pachypodium geayi*, and the rear of the library is framed by papyrus and bamboo. Succulents, bird of paradise, and additional varieties of palms stabilize the soil on the steep slope leading down to the golf course. Everything flourishes in the microclimate of Santa Monica Canyon, where a marine layer tempers summer heat and winter cold, and this explains the huge size of the fig trees, which were planted by the first settlers.

Pampas grass, yucca, aloe, Euphorbias, Dracaena, and other drought-resistant plants occupy the yard outside of the children's rooms, and water features at the front door and beside the pool provide a cooling murmur. At the far edge of the backyard is a bonsai pine—a solitary survivor from the demolished landscape. The plantings cascade and explode within a tightly controlled environment, playing off the color, texture and shape of river rock, Mexican blue stone, and crushed granite walkways. They serve as green sculpture, furnishing outdoor rooms.

"This garden is an oddity—like a seed dropped from an airplane," says Michael. "Suddenly there is tropical vegetation that never grew here before. Spare plants can be layered to look lush and dense, just as pared-down furniture can be grouped to achieve a richness of incident and detail." Looking through the house, there's an interplay of transparency and reflection, exuberance and sobriety, the natural and the manufactured. Foliage casts wavering shadows over the aluminum louvers. The roof beams are reflected in the pool, and those horizontal accents are complemented by a vertical obelisk that Michael designed in homage to those that Niemeyer included in other landscapes.

This harmonious ensemble would guarantee the house a place in the pantheon of modernism, but the integration of furniture, objects, books, and art with architecture raises the experience to a higher plane. It is a total work of art, in which the whole is much greater than the sum of the parts. "To me, a work of art is a creation through which we joyfully share in experiencing a bit of reality," wrote Gerrit Rietveld in 1919, and the Boyds enjoy that reality.

As the Boyds explain in their essays on chasing and living with modernism, the house is an expression of their way of life, in which ideas are as important as the physical presence of the container and its contents. In this, they are at one with the pioneers, who emphasized their social agenda as much as the formal language of design. In his diaries (published in English as *Berlin in Lights*), Count Harry Kessler, a progressive German aristocrat, describes a 1932 meeting with André Gide. He took the writer on a tour of a new Berlin housing estate, a humane modern complex that has survived seven decades of turmoil and is today cherished more than ever. Gide was duly impressed and lamented the backwardness of his own country. Why had the French lost their feeling for architecture, whereas in Germany it had blossomed forth? "To look on this architecture simply as architecture, art for art's sake so to speak, is to miss its point," Kessler responded. "It has to be understood as a new way of living, a new assessment of what life is for and how it should be lived. That holds good for architecture at any particular period and explains the hideous, fussy and ostentatious building at the turn of the century, reflecting precisely the vulgar ideals of the time."

For Michael, the moment of truth came in 1981, when he went to a Marcel Breuer exhibition at the Museum of Modern Art in New York and was swept away. It proved a revelation of how furniture and architecture can express similar ideas. As an art student at the University of California–Berkeley, he was already hooked on Malevich and Mondrian, unconsciously falling under their influence in doing his own work, and realizing how elusive was the perfection of scale. A love of furniture grew out of art, and he started buying Eames chairs in flea markets, long before they had acquired value for collectors. "My parents were two UCB English professors, my mother collected antiques, and my love of minimalism may be a reaction against the fuzzy macramé look of Berkeley," he recalls.

The Boyds cherish the economy of a great idea and believe that the patina or rust a piece acquires over the years gives it soul. Like many kids, Michael collected baseball cards and, later, guitars, but even then he instinctively went for rare

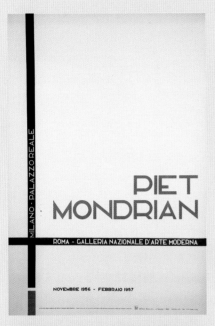

Piet Mondrian Exhibition poster issued by Editalia, Rome, 1956

Marcel Breuer Armchair (Model B-10) for Thonet, c. 1928

vintage items, in preference to new stuff. Gabrielle jokes that they've acquired "tons of minimalism," and the compulsion to collect is tempered only by their desire to focus on the most significant designs. "Often the prototype is experimental," Michael says. "I seek the oldest and best example of the design that went into production. These architects wanted to reach a mass public without compromising the integrity of their designs." Sometimes, he'll buy later versions, citing the Le Corbusier chairs that Heidi Weber made in Zurich in 1958–60, and the wood furniture of Prouvé and Perriand that Steph Simone produced in Paris in the 1950s and '60s as the best of their kind.

Their collection has evolved in response to the different houses they have owned, their means, and the opportunity to make new acquisitions. Though they shun fashion, their tastes have changed substantially over the past twenty years. There's been a shift from the ubiquitous classics of Mies and Le Corbusier, Aalto's Scroll and Rietveld's Red Blue chairs to lesser-known designs and designers. The emphasis on postwar American design has yielded to a focus on the first- and second-generation European modernists. They've gone back to the source, to the moment when an entirely new concept made its debut. The start date has receded to include proto modernists like Christopher Dresser, whose conical red vase—a purist version of a tajine cover—was made in 1870 as shining exception to the late-Victorian orgy of debased ornament.

The collection begins in Vienna in 1900 with Wagner, Loos, and Hoffmann, moves on to Germany in the 1920s, France in the 1930s and 1940s, and America and Italy in the two postwar decades. It's remarkable how the center of innovation shifts over the century, alighting in one country after another. Inevitably there are exceptions, and it's rewarding to discover secondary and tertiary designers who may have created one great piece in their lives, or an interesting variation on a theme. Erich Mendelsohn and J. J. P. Oud are justly celebrated for their buildings but few know that each did an extraordinary chair. The unifying principles are rigor and originality and the avoidance of clichés and sentimentality. Much as they love the Eameses, they find the child's plywood chair with a heart-shaped cutout to be uncomfortably cute. But there's an honored place for Carlo Mollino, the antirational Italian architect who sublimated his sexual fantasies in his expressive, erotic furniture. The cutoff is the early 1970s, to allow the inclusion of Verner Panton's plastic chairs and Frank Gehry's first experiments in cardboard.

"It's easier to identify the best of the past—the ephemeral fades away," observes Gabrielle. "It's hard to get a perspective on current work because there are so many factors in play." Michael sees himself as a custodian. "We can only hope to preserve a couple of houses, but we've saved many important chairs and books and helped them enjoy the recognition they deserve," he explains. "We are interested only in the progressive, not the trendy, fashionable, or bourgeois, and nearly all the designers we admire were architects."

Aesthetic and practical issues overlap. The monetary value of Prouvé's chairs has escalated sharply, but most were made for student dorms and were constructed to withstand hard use. Donald Judd's sharp-edged plywood furniture is as rigorous as his art, but his chairs are also put to use. Rietveld stuck a label on one of his early constructivist chairs which, roughly translated, reads "if you want to be comfortable, go to bed." The Boyds find their comfort in ergonomic postwar Danish modern.

Oscar Niemeyer Lounge chair for Mobilier de France, c. 1970

George Nelson Associates Marshmallow sofa for Herman Miller, 1956

In fact, many of the chairs are more liveable than they first appear, and the Boyds prefer to move around and experience different ways of sitting, not collapse into a lounger and doze off after dinner. In this house, the past comes alive and you can imagine friends gathering at the Bauhaus, in Rietveld's atelier in Utrecht, or at the SAS Royal Hotel in Copenhagen, to marvel at the latest breakthrough and wriggle around. It's back to the future; to the springtime freshness of modernism when Lily Reich was working with Mies and Charlotte Perriand with Le Corbusier, going where no one had gone before. The concepts are as provocative as ever, but they've also acquired a historical resonance.

"It's very inspiring," says Gabrielle. "We can be scurrying around to get the boys off to school and realize what an impact a beautiful object or detail can have on your day."

What links these four contemporaries, as well as Mies and Le Corbusier, Wagner and Hoffmann, Aalto and the Eameses is the originality and sweep of their creativity. All but Prouvé (who was a natural) came to design by way of architecture, then regarded as the mother of the arts. All understood the big picture and the ways people are affected by space, light, materials, and colors. That put their furnishings (what Le Corbusier called "equipment for living") on a solid foundation, serving function not fashion. These formgivers were uninterested in style or applied decoration, and, though they often failed to win popular acceptance or the mass production many craved, their designs appear as timeless today as when they made their debut.

For the Boyds, the goal is to acquire significant variations on these themes of structure, shape, and support, and explore the ways in which they relate together. The house provides a warm and tranquil environment in which these ideas can live and breathe. Each element relates to its neighbors to create a symphony of forms that is also a functional setting for everyday life. The sturdiest pieces are placed in the living room where everyone can use them, while the more delicate pieces are reserved for the library, or are placed on shelves in the archive. Selection and juxtaposition were thoughtfully pondered. In contrast to the rigorous chronology and thematic groupings of MoMA's design collection, periods, styles, and shapes are scrambled to achieve a lively interplay.

Organic plays off mechanic, early off late, sybaritic off austere. As in yoga, the arrangement is not a quest for perfection, but rather the act of perfecting; adding, subtracting, and shifting pieces to achieve provocative relationships. Sometimes, a single shape stands out. The circular forms of a Noguchi stool, a Frederick Kiesler table, George Nelson's Marshmallow sofa, and Serge Mouille's floor lamp draw the eye across the room and through the glass to the stacked cones of the Architectural Pottery totem beside the pool and fireworks explosion of the yucca bushes. The hierarchy of scale ascends from a Hoffmann bud vase or African mask, through the chairs and cabinets to the house, which is the largest object in the collection.

In the living room, seating by Niemeyer and Prouvé holds center stage. Both offer comfortable support while demonstrating how form can serve function in radically different ways. The Brazilian joined two black leather cushions with a curved steel spring that moves with your body and conjures pleasant images of samba in the Rio Carnival and shapely young women on Copacabana beach. Those images were certainly in Niemeyer's mind as he created these chairs during his late 1960s

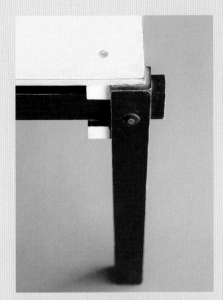

exile in Paris and employed them in the lobby of his headquarters building for the French Communist Party. Quite unromantically they supported the butts of gray apparatchiks, earnestly debating the minutiae of doctrine or strategy for the next strike.

Prouvé, by contrast, was an undoctrinaire socialist who treated his employees as companions and shareholders in an atelier that made extraordinary furniture for ordinary people. The Visiteur armchair was introduced in 1942, a frugal product of Nazi-occupied France, comprising a back and seat of slatted wood supported on metal rods that are bent to provide legs and support wooden armrests. The slats could be upholstered or covered with cushions, and the chair appeared in several different versions over the next decade. Beauty was not a word Prouvé used, and it's unlikely that the female form had any place in his thinking about design, but the simple forms of this chair have a grace and flow that lift it above the merely functional. The delight resides in the way the materials are handled and that same unpretentious, foursquare character informs the demountable Standard side chairs that are grouped around the Prouvé dining table beside the kitchen. The table accommodates laptops and dinner parties as comfortably as the Alexandre Noll wood jugs and peasant-like pottery by George Jouve, contemporaries of the designer who shared some of his rough-hewn sensibility.

Beside the entry, and serving as a room divider, is a freestanding steel and wood storage unit that Prouvé created in collaboration with Charlotte Perriand in 1953 for the Maison de Mexique at the Cité Universitaire in Paris. The painter Sonia Delaunay advised on the colors, and this rugged combination of shelves and cabinets makes a fascinating contrast with the delicate units that Charles and Ray Eames produced a few years earlier. No two pieces could be so alike in content or so different in expression. A Perriand stool and a low Eames table of the same vintage provide another example of how designers proceed on parallel tracks and then move off in different directions.

Rietveld is represented by an example of the Elling buffet, crafted in a limited quantity under the master's supervision in the 1960s. The original was a unique piece, made in 1919, and subsequently destroyed by fire. It's a marvel of constructivism, in which every element is separately expressed, while remaining as unified a work of art as the *Untitled (Swiss Box)* sculpture of Donald Judd that keeps it company. Its delicate texture and precise joinery compel you to open every drawer and flap. The kitchen also suggests a walk-in constructivist sculpture with its cabinets suspended on steel rods and the shimmering backdrop of translucent glass sliders that pull in light and the shadows of bamboo from the side garden.

While admiring these landmarks of modern design, you notice the many unfamiliar pieces, which include a pair of armchairs framed in lacquered steel and upholstered in cheetah fur. They were designed in 1928 by Robert Mallet-Stevens, the French architect, whose modernist principles were tempered by the preferences of high society. Here, too, is a chair by André Bloc and stools by Perriand and Le Corbusier. Together, they provide an anthology of French midcentury modernism. "It's intriguing to juxtapose an anonymous piece with one that has a pedigree and a third that's primitive and find the through line," says Michael. "Everything has to relate and not be just a beautiful thing on display. It's a collage; good goes with good, and if a piece isn't inspiring it doesn't hold its place very long."

In the reading room above the library, the focus is on sophisticated French and Italian pieces, precisely placed. A standout is the chair that Jean Burkhalter created for the 1937 Paris Exposition, and is still in immaculate condition. Its jute webbing is supported on a springy tubular metal frame that resembles an unfolded paper clip and has the expressive, hand-drawn quality of zen calligraphy. There's a cubist desk and stool by Pierre Chareau, plus a side table he designed for a chess club in the south of France. The weight of a Prouvé sofa contrasts with the taut springiness of René Herbst's Sandows chair, in which elastic cords are attached to a patinated metal frame in a radical experiment of 1930. From Italy, there are two whimsical designs of the 1950s: Carlo Mollino's split-back café chair of 1947, and Gio Ponti's glass-topped coffee table with a white-enamelled base that suggests (in a play on the designer's name) a suspension bridge. The raised door to the bathroom was designed by Perriand for the Maison du Bresil at the Cité Universitaire but might as easily have come from an ocean liner.

Each of the rooms in the side wing has its own distinctive character. The Boyds' sons picked a favorite side chair for their bedrooms; Sam chose a Panton and Henry an Eames. The master bedroom is dominated by Yayoi Kusama's *Infinity Net* of 1959, but most of the furnishings are postwar American classics. Nelson's Coconut chair share the space with a Noguchi rocking stool and marble-topped side tables that Alexander Girard designed for the offices of Braniff Airlines, a short-lived company that embodied high style in the 1960s. Glass sliders open up to a Case Study terrace equipped with Van Keppel Green chairs of tubular steel and marine cord, and sculptural pieces by Architectural Pottery.

The media room acknowledges the twenty-first century in its plasma screen, but the posters recall classic American and European movies that the whole family prefers over most current offerings. The Rudolph couch is the one piece the Boyds brought from their New York house, and it sits well with a metal and rope Hans Wegner Flagline chair. Gabrielle has a light-filled office opening onto the pocket garden beside the entry. A German edition of Nelson's wall storage unit, with an impeccably engineered aluminum frame and enameled steel shelves, complements Prouvé's Compass desk, which was designed for an office in Brazzaville during the French colonial administration. A De Stijl tapestry by Theo Van Doesburg provides a bold splash of color. In the corridor that links these rooms, vintage Man Ray photographs are juxtaposed with enough African spears to stage a battle.

Michael's inner sanctum is the library—a book-lined retreat with a central table that is piled high with objects and paper. Chairs and stacked posters occupy the narrow space between and the first impression is one of overwhelming congestion—exactly what the modernists took issue with. There's a famous poster for the Weissenhofsiedlung of 1927 in Stuttgart in which a claustrophobic Victorian interior is slashed in red and the slogan reads, "This is not how to live!" It's part of the Boyd collection, along with some of the best graphics of the twentieth century, catalogues, and volumes by and about every major modern architect, artist, and designer.

"My parents were professors—one in linguistic philosophy, and the other in Victorian English literature—and every wall of our home was covered in books," Michael recalls. At age ten, he hated them, but, after blowing a chunk of his first college allowance on a seventy-five-dollar book about Noguchi, he realized

he was hooked, too. He built a huge collection of bargains at Moe's, Cody's, and Shakespeare and Co. in Berkeley, at William Stout (which was across the street from his music recording studio in San Francisco) and all over Europe. "Once I had a book on an artist or designer I liked, I wanted to know what others had written," he explains. "I use these books for reference, to remind me of things I've seen, and as a surrogate for work I cannot afford, by artists such as Ad Reinhardt, Barnett Newman and Piero Manzoni."

The titles, recently culled to about 10,000, are obsessively ordered and a few are propped flat in front or on a display rack with related objects, like altars to favorite saints—though the feeling is entirely secular. The central table is a distillation of the collection and a series of overlapping narratives on different aspects of modernism. Clocks by Peter Behrens and Marianne Brandt, a Piet Zwart triangular can and a De Stijl-style sculpture from the Art Institute of Chicago, complement books and pamphlets with boldly graphic covers by El Lissitzky, Hoffmann, Le Corbusier, and Karel Teige.

Books, art, furniture, plants, and architecture: this house demonstrates the potential of modernism to combine the practical and exotic, the sensory and the intellectual in one rewarding package. It incorporates some of the greatest work of the twentieth century but it's intensely personal: the choices that two people made over twenty-five years. It challenges the widely shared belief that modernism is too spare and Spartan to win popular acceptance.

Niemeyer's house comes at the end of a brief postwar honeymoon in which modernism was presented as something humane, rational, and stripped down; a model for how everybody might live. It is an artifact from a vanished era, a vision of a future that was never to be. It brings together a host of small-scale experiments, some of which have endured or influenced the best designers of today. And yet, though the volume of creativity and public acceptance has grown exponentially, something important has been lost. In architecture and interior design, idealism has faded, and modernism is often no more than a strategy for expressing status and material wealth. The Boyds are surrounded by treasures, but they live in an unpretentious way, seeking to balance the vision with reality.

On this and the succeeding seven pages we present a study in frustration, the defeat of a fine, imaginative design by paralyzing building regulations and their dogged, immovable enforcers. The architect's sketches and accompanying notes document the development by Oscar Niemeyer — principal architect of Brasilia — of his concept for a house situated on a bluff overlooking a verdant country club with the Santa Monica Mountains as a backdrop.

With the magnificent view uppermost in his mind, Niemeyer visualized the house on two levels: the major living areas at lot level and bedrooms recessed into the face of the bluff, thus opening them to the view also. The first of the original solutions (model photo at right, drawing on page 22) places living and garden areas as a unit beneath an uninhibited, free-flowing roof that is characteristic of a number of Niemeyer's house designs. The second of the original proposals (site plan on page 23, additional plans and elevation bottom of page 25) places a glass-enclosed, rectangular living room athwart the site. Bedroom area floor plan for both solutions are on page 24.

For some incomprehensible reason, the local building codes prohibit below-grade bedrooms (reportedly officials fear subterranean rooms will be turned into rental units; this in an area with homes ranging in price from $100,000 to $200,000!) and the first two solutions were struck down. After flirting with a two-story plan (top of page 25; vetoed by the client), the final compromise solution on pages 26 and 27 became a more conventional — but no more workable — adaptation of the second site plan. All rooms are at grade level. Of the bedrooms, only the owners' opens to the view.

Niemeyer, who has never been allowed into the United States for reasons which are the residue of a period of political hysteria, explains to the client in a letter accompanying the final proposal that the favored free-form roof must be discarded since it would lose its lightness if used over the larger area of the new plan. Instead, he suggests that the walls of fixed glass enclosing the living areas be hung from a number of concrete rafters cantilevering from two large concrete beams.

Niemeyer's letter to the client (slightly abridged):

"Dear Joseph Strick

"Yesterday, in the vespers of my departure for Ghana — Africa — I got your letter together with the plan . . .

"I have examined the plan and felt that in spite of the mess which precedes any trip, I should try another solution and especially I should warn you that the proposed modification diversifies the original idea which locates

(Continued on page 28)

OSCAR NIEMEYER

PROJECT FOR A HOUSE IN SANTA MONICA, CALIFORNIA,

Oscar Niemeyer Strick House, Arts + Architecture, September 1964

the solution must consider:

   ① the splendid view opening to the back of the lot

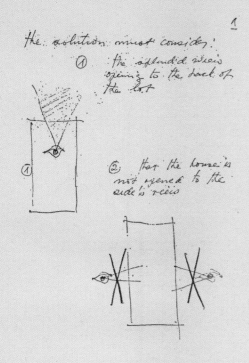

   ② that the house is not opened to the side's view

within this program, I find that the best solution would be the one in which the bed rooms and living could take advantage of the view

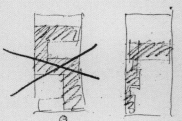

3 – In order to not reduce the free (garden) spaces, an essential item in my opinion, I have left the lot level exclusively for the living, dining room, gardens, service area, etc, being the bed rooms located in another level

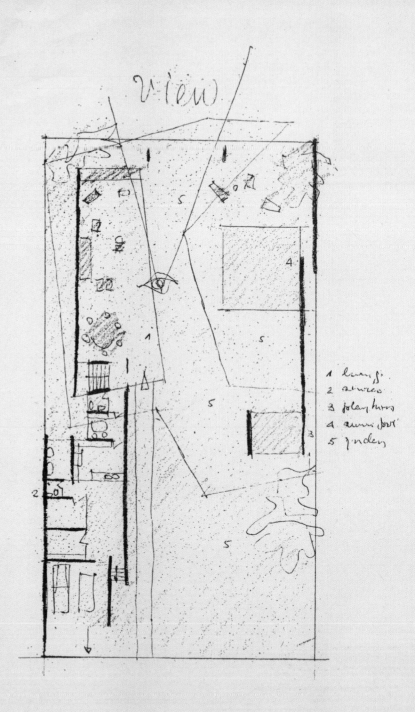

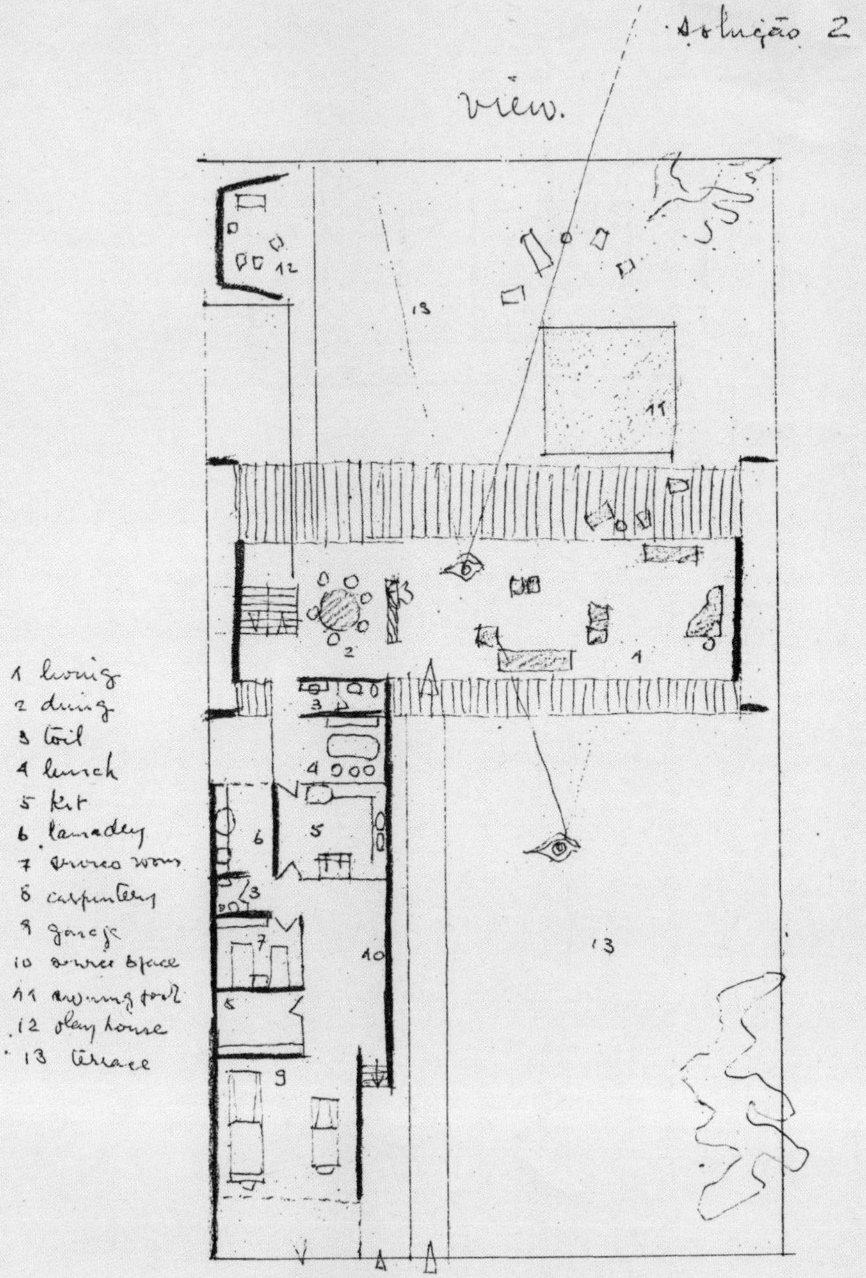

Solução 2

view.

1 living
2 dining
3 toil
4 lunch
5 kit
6 laundry
7 service room
8 carpentry
9 garage
10 service space
11 awning tool
12 play house
13 terrace

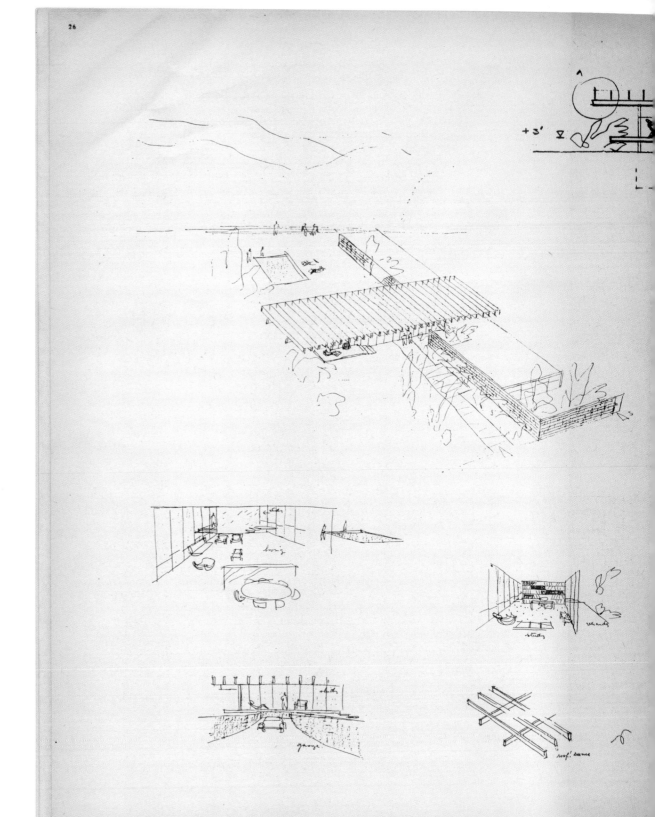

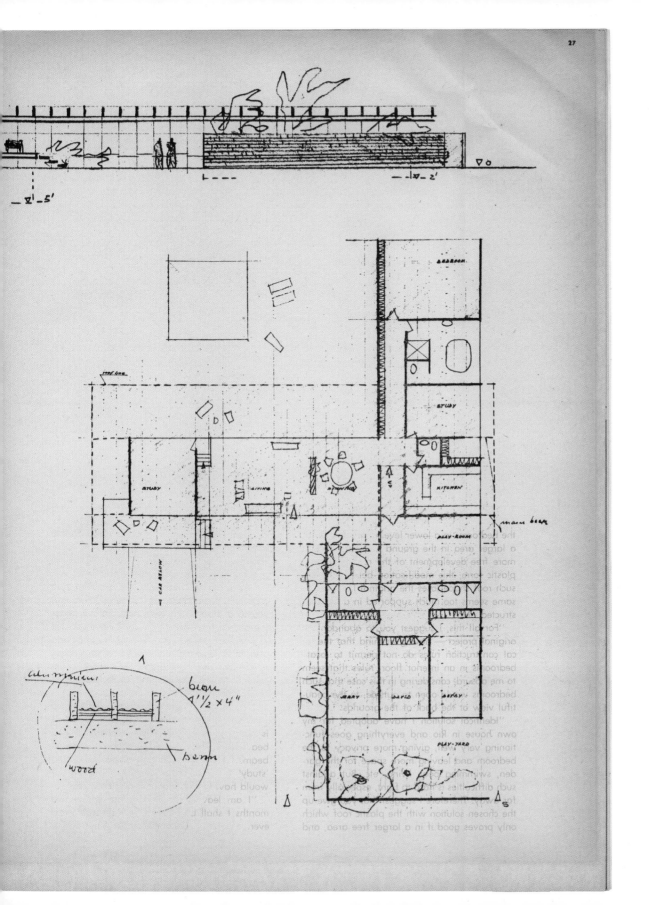

the bedrooms in a lower level in order to profit a larger area in the ground and permitting a more free development of the roof in a more plastic form; this modification being adopted, such roof shape loses the original lightness as same seems too much supported in a big constructed area.

"For all this, I suggest you to abandon the original project — having in mind that the local construction rules do not permit to locate bedrooms in an inferior floor, rules that seem to me absurd, considering in this case that such bedrooms would open to outside, to the beautiful view at the back of the grounds.

"Identical solution I have adopted for my own house in Rio and everything goes functioning very well, giving more privacy to the bedroom and leaving more space for the garden, swimming pool, living, etc. But against such difficulties is hard to fight, especially from far away. Therefore I suggest that you give up the chosen solution with the plastic roof which only proves good if in a larger free area, and

to direct the solution for your house to a more simple drawing, maintaining, as it is indispensable (you wish no stairs), everything in the ground within the adequate proportions.

"As I am worried with the problem and especially the idea that my cooperation brought you to a plan which does not approve under the architectural point of view, I have decided to write and tell you honestly what I think and also, in spite of the few time I had, to propose a different solution more in accordance to the ground dimensions and to the rule impositions of your country.

"The plan that I am sending you respects the functional lines of the 'sketch' sent to me. It is simple, and constructive, economical and beautiful. The roof would be made of concrete beams, aluminum tiles and wood lining. The 'study' would be more joined to the living but would have an independent outside access . . .

"I am leaving for Ghana, but within two months I shall be back at your disposition as ever.   Oscar Niemeyer 13/2/64"

Charlotte Perriand, Jean Prouvé, and **Sonia Delaunay** Wall unit for the Maison du Méxique, 1953
André Bloc Bellvue chair, 1951

James Prestini Turned wood bowls, c. 1950 **Alexandre Noll** Wood bowl, c. 1950 **Christopher Dresser** Ceramic vessel, c. 1880 **Finn Juhl** Teak bowl, c. 1954 **Man Ray** *Halteres—Square Dumb Bells,* 1944/45 African footed stool **Alvar Aalto** Free-form glass, c. 1930 **Alexandre Noll** Sycamore bowl, c. 1950 **Stig Lindberg** Veckla vases for Gustavsberg, 1950s **Finn Juhl** Teak bowl, c. 1954 Architectural pottery vessels, c. 1950 Japanese bent plywood lunchbox, c. 1880 **Gio Ponti** Fire-enameled copper bowl, 1950s

44

Living room (left to right):

Robert Mallet-Stevens Pair of lounge chairs, c. 1928

Charles and Ray Eames Prototype for the dowel-legged side table, c. 1950

Charlotte Perriand Pair of stools, 1950s

Oscar Niemeyer Pair of chairs and ottomans for Mobilier de France, c. 1970

Jean Prouvé Pair of Visiteur chairs, 1942

John McLaughlin *Untitled*, oil on masonite, 1957

Man Ray *Le Torse Tournant*, bronze sculpture, 1959

Marcel Breuer Nesting tables for Isokon, 1936

Philip Johnson with **Richard Kelly** Bronze floor lamp, 1954

Charles and Ray Eames Surfboard table for Herman Miller, c. 1950

50

In background (left to right):

Serge Mouille Floor lamp, 1953

Frederick Kiesler Cast aluminum free-form nesting tables, 1935

Donald Judd Galvanized steel armchair, 1993

Burgoyne Diller *First Theme*, oil on canvas, 1959–60

George Nelson Associates Thin Edge cabinet for Herman Miller, c. 1950

Serge Mouille Hanging light fixture, 1958

André Bloc Bellvue chair procuction model, 1951; Bellvue chair prototype model, 1950

André Bloc Bellvue chair prototype model, 1950
Stig Lindberg Veckla vases for Gustavsberg, c. 1950
Burgoyne Diller First Theme, oil on canvas, 1959–60
George Nelson Associates Thin Edge cabinet for Herman Miller, c. 1950

Kitchen (left to right):

Arne Jacobsen Stainless barware for Stelton, 1967

Jean Prouvé Stool, c. 1950

Mathieu Matégot Tray, c. 1950

Pierre Chareau Bar stools, c. 1930

Eero Saarinen Tulip stools for Knoll, 1956

George Nelson Associates Ball clock for Howard Miller, 1956

Jacques Adnet Wine caddy, 1930s

Wood objects by **Alexandre Noll**
Ceramic objects by **Georges Jouve**

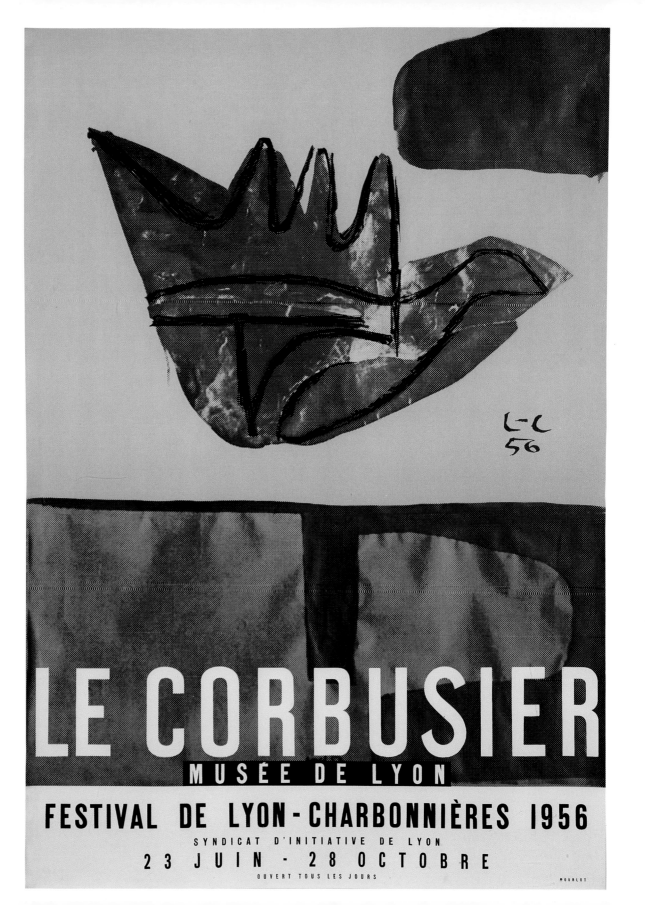

Finn Juhl Teak bowls for Kay Bojesen, 1950s

Le Corbusier Offset lithograph for Musée de Lyon, 1956

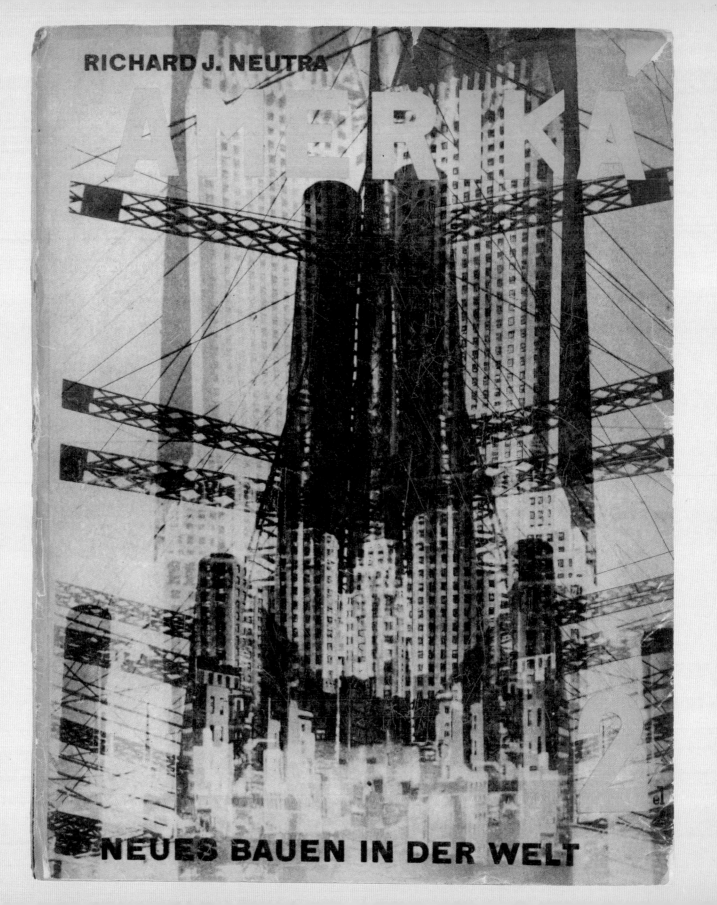

1

MSA

mezinárodní
soudobá architektura

sborník
1929

architektura a urbanismus · architekt a konstruktér · industrielní
stavební metody · dům a palác · jak se má bydlet ? · stavitelství
budoucnosti · město zítřku ·

stavební tvorba v Anglii, Belgii, ČSR, Francii, Holandsku, Italii, Japonsku,
Jugoslavii, Maďarsku, Německu, SSSR, ve Švýcařích a v U.S.A.

L'architecture internationale d'aujourd'hui
Internationale Architektur der Gegenwart

Odeon

ODEON PRAHA 1930

MSA 2

moderní architektura
v československu

karel teige

Karel Teige, MSA 1 *Internationale Architektur der Gegenwart,* 1929
Karel Teige, MSA 2 *Internationale Architektur der Gegenwart,* 1930

Das Neue Frankfurt vols. 1, 2, 3, and 7, 1926/27

Frederick Kiesler Cover design for his book *Contemporary Art Applied to the Store and Its Display*, 1930

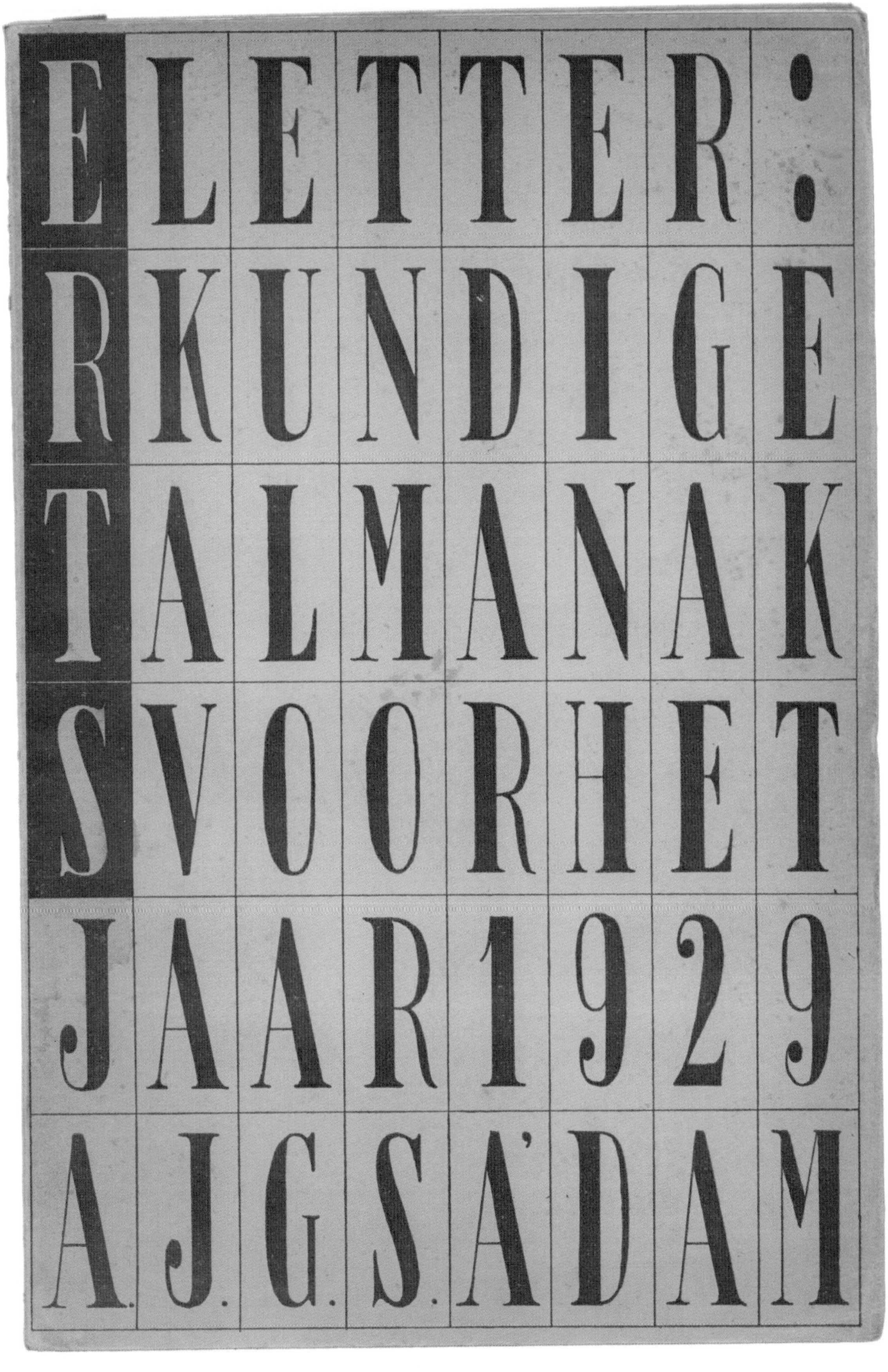
ELETTER:
RKUNDIGE
TALMANAK
SVOORHET
JAAR1929
A.J.G.S.A'DAM

Gerrit Rietveld Cover design for *ERTS*, 1929

El Lissitsky Cover design for *Wendingen*, 1921

Library Table (clockwise from top left):
Marianne Brandt Tray for Ruppel, c. 1930
Josef Hoffmann Candlestick for Wiener Werkstätte, c. 1905
Piet Zwart Tin for Brenoline, c. 1930
Peter Behrens Clock for AEG, 1909

Karel Teige Cover design for *Avantgardní Architektura*, 1936

R. J. Neutra, F. Casinello, 1968

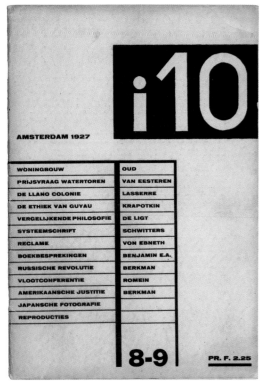

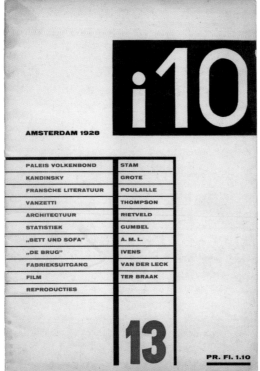

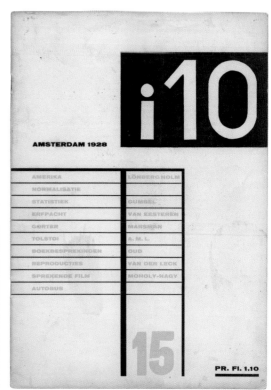

neues
bauen
in
berlin

EIN FÜHRER MIT 168 BILDERN

AUSSTELLUNG

Das Werk des Wiener Architekten (1841-1918)
Ausstellung
im Hessischen Landesmuseum in Darmstadt
vom 23. November 1963-2. Februar 1964

geöffnet:		geschlossen:
Dienstag bis Samstag	10—17 Uhr	montags
Mittwoch, außerdem	19—21 Uhr	1. Weihnachtsfeiertag
Sonntag	10—13 Uhr	1. Januar

OTTO WAGNER

Adolf Loos Bentwood and cane side chair for the Café Museum, Vienna, c. 1898

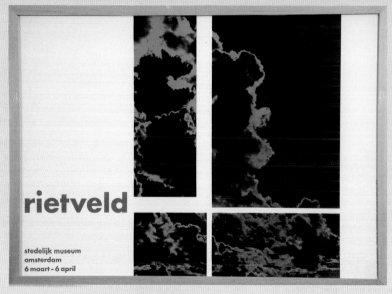

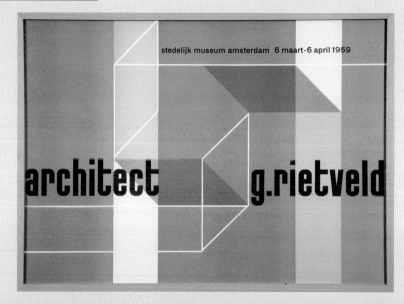

Willem Sandberg Triptych graphics for Stedelijk Museum, 1959

Gerrit Rietveld Moolenbeek Zig-Zag chair, 1942
Christopher Dresser Letter rack, c. 1880
Frank Lloyd Wright Usonian table, c. 1950

Gerrit Rietveld Zig-Zag chair, 1934

Piet Zwart Design for *Kamergymnastiek Voor Iedereen*, c. 1935
Piet Zwart Design for *Radio*, c.1935

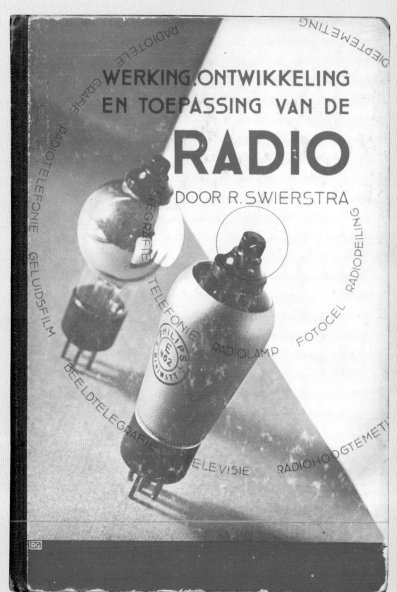

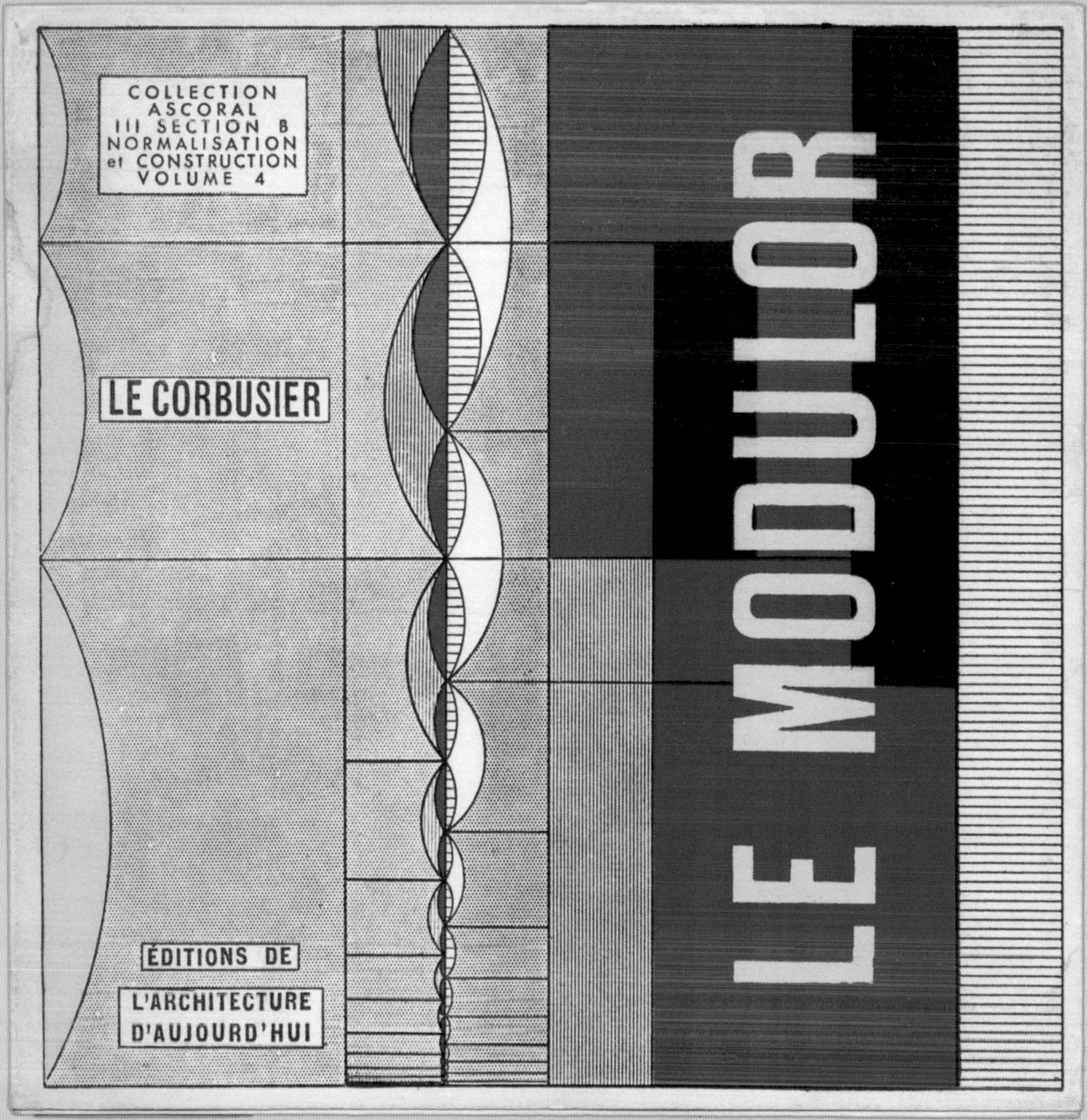

COLLECTION
ASCORAL
III SECTION B
NORMALISATION
et CONSTRUCTION
VOLUME 4

LE CORBUSIER

ÉDITIONS DE

L'ARCHITECTURE

D'AUJOURD'HUI

LE MODULOR

Le Corbusier *Le Modulor*, 1954

Otto Wagner Stool from the main banking room of the Austrian Post Office Savings Bank, Vienna, c.1906

Josef Hoffmann, L.W. Rochowanski, 1950

LW
ROCHOWANSKI
*
JOSEF
HOFFMANN

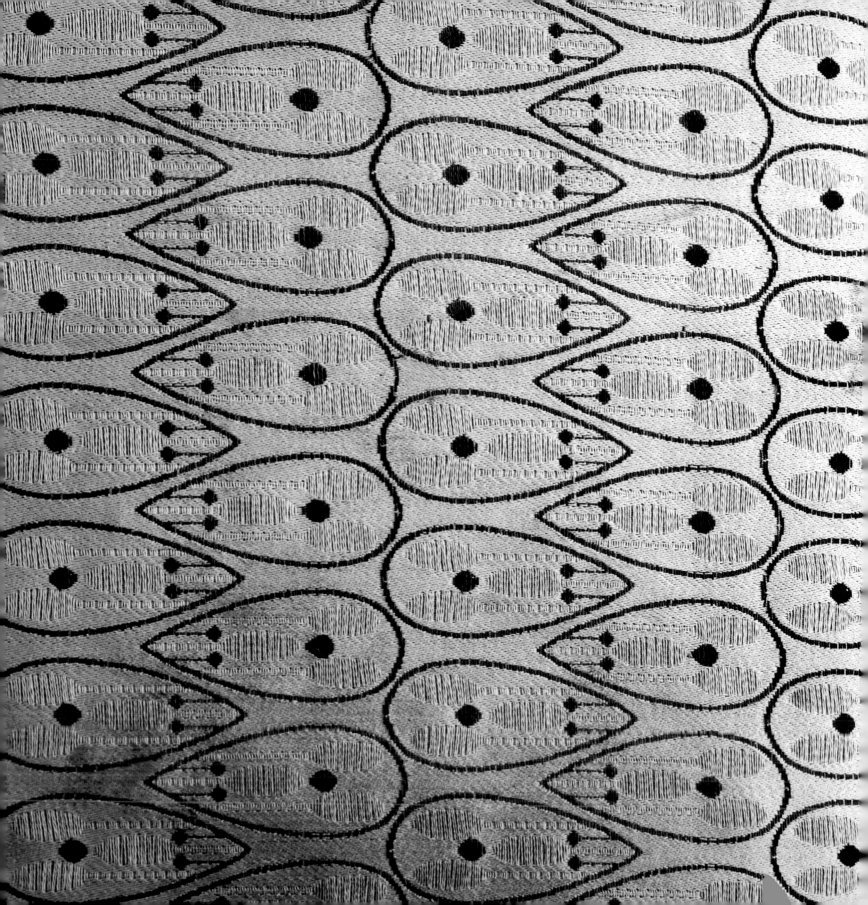

Josef **Hoffmann** Stool for J. & J. Kohn, c. 1902

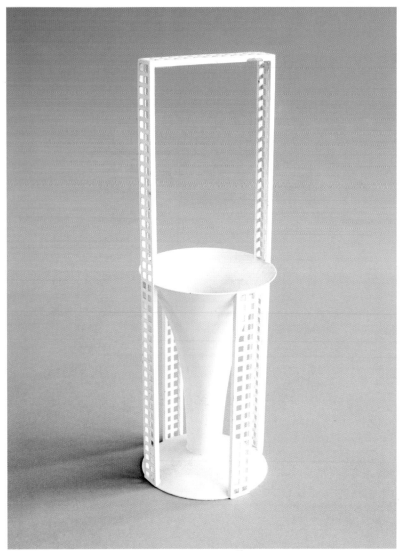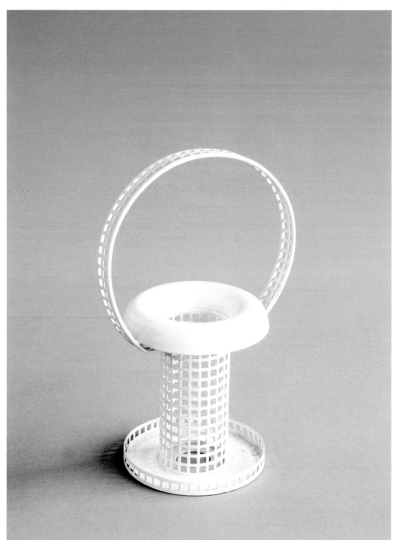

 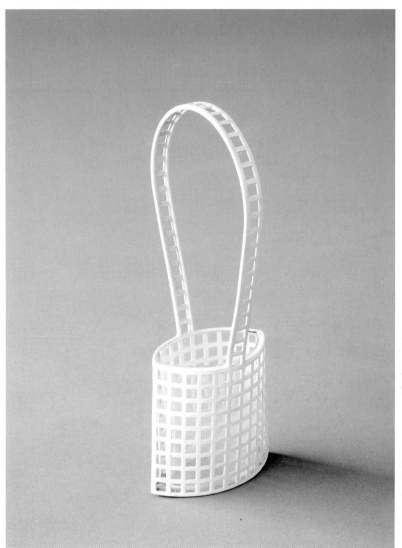

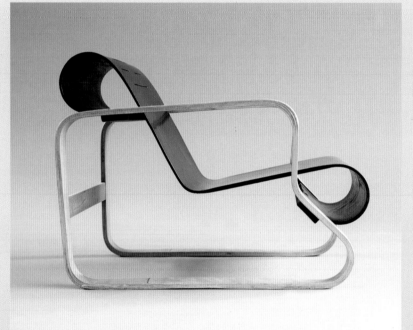

Alvar Aalto:

Side chair for Artek (model 2), 1932/33
Paimio armchair for Finmar (model 41), 1931/32
Lounge chair for Artek (model 34), 1932
Lounge chair for Artek (model 31), 1931/32

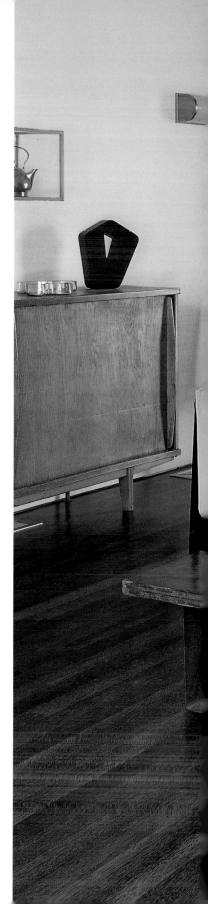

Reading room (left to right):

Pierre Chareau Side table, c. 1927

Jean Prouvé Banquette, 1954

Carlo Scarpa Glass vase for Venini, 1936

Donald Judd *Untitled* Plywood sculpture, 1978

Eileen Gray Stool for E-1027, 1931/32

Gio Ponti Brass vessel for Christofle, c. 1958

Jean Prouvé Bridge director's chair c. 1950

Jean Burkhalter Armchair for the Paris Exposition, 1937

Moderne Architectuur! J.G. Wattjes, 1927

Left to right:

Jean Prouvé Cabinet, c 1930

Gerrit Rietveld Hanfor hanging glass cabinet, retailed by Metz & Co., 1926

Christopher Dresser Decanter for Hukin & Heath, 1881

Christopher Dresser Sugar bowl for Hukin & Heath, c. 1885

Alvar Aalto Free-form glass, c. 1930

Peter Behrens Teapot for AEG (Allgemeine Elektrizitäts-Gesellschaft), c. 1905

Jean Arp *Heads or Tails*, bronze sculpture, 1959

Jean Prouvé Banquette 1954
Carlo Scarpa Glass vase for Venini, 1936
Eileen Gray Stool for E-1027, 1931/32
Donald Judd Untitled Plywood sculpture, 1978

Pierre Chareau Desk, c. 1927
Pierre Chareau Stool (model no. SN 3), c. 1927
Donald Judd *Untitled* Galvanized steel single stack sculpture, 1965
Inkwell attributed to **Gerhard Marcks**, c. 1930
J. J. P. Oud Giso table lamp (model 405) for Gispen, 1928

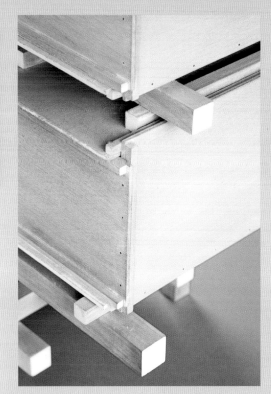

Gerrit Rietveld (1888–1964) designed more than 350 pieces of furniture and completed one hundred buildings, but his reputation rests on the magical little house he designed for Truus Schroeder-Schraeder in his native city of Utrecht and on a handful of pieces that were reconstructed in the 1950s for a series of exhibitions. Later, sanitized versions of the Red Blue and Zig-Zag chairs and the Brugman end table were reissued by Cassina, and were then pirated. As Paul Overy has observed, "Examples that Rietveld constructed himself are often quite roughly made and crudely jointed, as if to modify the austerity of the designs, although it is clear from the execution of some of his pre-1918 furniture that he was a skilled and expert cabinetmaker as was his assistant Gerard van de Groenekan." (Complete Rietveld Furniture, 1993) That roughness is exactly what the Boyds most love: the mark of spontaneous creation, of assembling a piece quickly by hand before the inspiration wanes.

Though Rietveld was a member of De Stijl, he made sparing use of the primary colors that are the Dutch group's signature. The Red/Blue chair began life as an unfinished wood construction in 1918, and the colored version appeared five years later, after Rietveld had used bright colors on a children's cart and wheelbarrow. What interested him most were structure, spatiality, and purity of expression. "I made chairs intended to parallel the level reached by architecture [at that time]," he wrote. The open compositions of boards and struts with cantilevered arms do suggest a building in miniature, and the Schroeder house with its retractable screens functions very much like an oversized piece of furniture.

Art Intensifies and expands our faculties of perception and enlarges our view of the world. — GERRIT RIETVELD

Gerrit Rietveld
Detail of sideboard, 19
Crate easy chair, 1934

Top: Stained wood high back armchair, 1924
Bottom: Berlin chair, 1923

Top to bottom:
Sideboard, designed 1919
Harrenstein hanging glass cabinet for Metz & Co., 1926
Child's wheelbarrow, 1923

Clockwise from top left:
Moolenbeek Zig-Zag chair, 1942
Beugelstoel for Metz & Co., 1927
Hoegestoel, 1919
Zig-Zag armchair with perforated back, 1932
Militar chair, 1923
Beugelstoel (low version) for Metz & Co., 1928

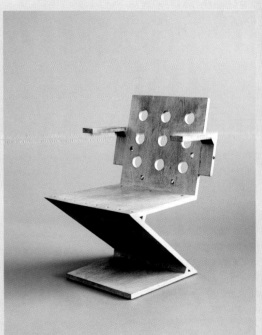

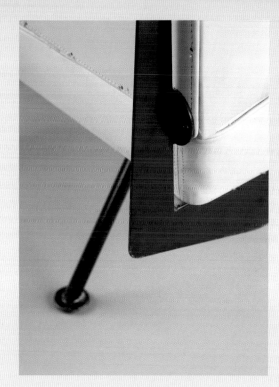

Like Rietveld, whose father crafted traditional furniture, **Jean Prouvé** (1901–1984) learned the skill of ironworking from his father and other metalworkers. As an artisan, self-taught engineer, and builder in the French city of Nancy, he was a hands-on innovator, welding sheet metal for furniture and buildings. He established an atelier in 1923 and bubbled over with invention until he lost control of his factory in the early 1950s. Furniture was a problem-solving exercise; the consistent goal was to achieve maximum utility with a minimum of materials at the lowest possible cost. His chairs, tables, cabinets, and swinging lights were produced in quantity for schools and universities, and the revenue subsidized his experiments in prefabrication. Prototypes of his Tropical House were shipped to French West Africa and flown back to France fifty years later to be restored and widely exhibited. To build his own house in Nancy he salvaged metal door and window components from the factory.

Le Corbusier declared that Prouvé "combined the soul of an engineer with that of an architect" (Jean Prouvé, 2002), but—since he lacked professional qualifications—such appreciation was rare in his lifetime. Since then, his public esteem has skyrocketed, and battered furnishings and wall panels fetch dizzying prices at auction. He is finally receiving his due as an intuitive genius. "Never design anything that cannot be made," was his mantra, and his strong, simple pieces are imbued with the personality of a skilled artisan who sketched, mocked-up, and refined every design himself before putting it into production. He cared nothing for fashion or social acceptance, and his furniture has a timeless appeal.

There is no difference between the construction of an item of furniture and that of a house. —JEAN PROUVÉ

Top: Bar stool, c. 1950
Bottom: Standard chair (wood version), c. 1950

Clockwise from top left:
Antony lounge chair, 1954
With Charlotte Perriand. Free-form table, c. 1950
Bridge Director's armchair, c. 1950
Standard chair (aluminum version) 1950

Clockwise from top left:
Standard chair, c. 1950
Visiteur chair, 1942
Demountable standard chair, c.1950
Banquette, 1954

MARCEL BREUER

Hungarian-born **Marcel Breuer** (1902–1981) was inspired by Rietveld's early experiments in wood, but his eureka moment reportedly came in 1925 in Dessau, while he was learning to ride a bicycle. Impressed by the strength and lightness of the steel tubing of the handlebars, he bent and soldered that material to create the first tubular metal chair. Mies and Mart Stam picked up on the idea even before Breuer had perfected the Wassily armchair (named for his Bauhaus colleague, Wassily Kandinsky, who was an early fan). As J. Stewart Johnson observed in *Marcel Breuer: Furniture and Interiors* (1981), "bent tubular steel was th e ideal material for modernist furniture . . . strong, lightweight, easily portable, and inexpensive to produce . . . it looked new; not only was it machine-made, it looked machine made."

Over the next few years, Breuer designed several other iconic chairs that have been widely copied. Furniture, he wrote in 1928, "is no longer massive, monumental, apparently rooted to the ground, or actually built-in. Instead, it is broken up airily, sketched into the room, as it were; it impedes neither movement nor the view through the room. . . . Metal furniture is intended to be nothing but a necessary apparatus for contemporary life." Comments of this kind were bound to fan a widely held prejudice that tubular steel was more suited to the hospital than the home. Bulky armchairs and sofas have retained their popular appeal up to the present. Breuer went on to create an elegant aluminum chaise that was translated into laminated wood for Isokon during his brief exile in London. Ironically, as an architect practicing in the U.S., he gave up furniture design to create buildings that became increasingly massive and monumental.

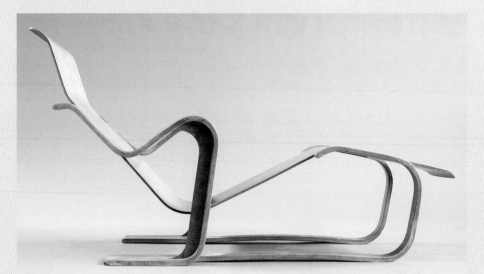

Furniture is no longer massive, monumental, apparently rooted to the ground, or actually built-in. Instead, it is broken up airily, sketched into the room, as it were. MARCEL BREUER

Detail of basket drawer unit for Thonet, c. 1930

Bent plywood chaise for Isokon, 1936

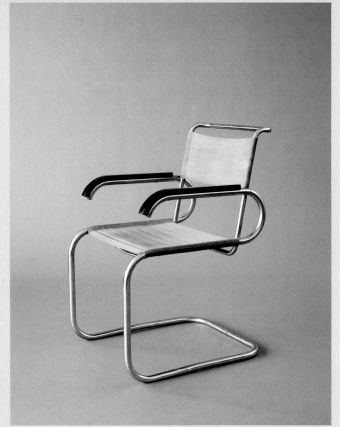

  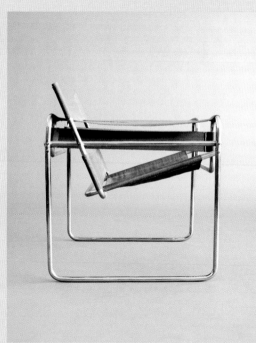

Clockwise from top left
Side chair For Thonet (Model B-33), 1928
Stool for Thonet (Model B-9), 1928/29
Basket drawer unit for Thonet, c. 1930
First version open-back Wassily club chair for
Thonet, 1925
Slatted armchair, 1922-24
Club chair for Thonet (Model B-3), c.1930

Top: Aluminum slatted chair for Embru, 1932-34
Bottom: Nesting tables for Thonet (model B-9), 1925/26

Arne Jacobsen (1902–1971) was a late bloomer who produced most of his iconic designs in his fifties, and then looked forward to a tranquil retirement as a gardener. He was a bourgeois amid the bohemians and radicals of the modern movement, a formalist with little interest in changing society and a perfectionist who created almost every chair and object for specific projects. Christopher Mount calls him "a devoted believer in controlling the 'total environment'—no detail was too minor for him to address." His architecture was cool and orthogonal: The curtain-walled slab tower atop a podium of the SAS Royal Hotel in Copenhagen drew on the Lever Building in New York. In contrast, the sensuously curved furniture was inspired by nature and the Scandinavian craft tradition, and was part of an organic trend that emerged in the 1940s, as exemplified by the work of the Eameses and Eero Saarinen. In designing the Egg chair, Jacobsen worked like a sculptor, carving models until he was satisfied with the form, a radically different approach to the constructivist technique of his predecessors.

The Ant—a lightweight, molded plywood stacking chair with three tubular metal legs—was designed in 1952 for a pharmaceutical company's cafeteria; today there may be more Ants in circulation than there are Danes. Still more successful was the Series 7 stacking chair, which may be the most popular chair of the century, though mostly in the form of cheap copies. Jacobsen's masterpiece was the SAS Hotel—though all the interiors except the legendary room 606 have been replaced. What survived were the Egg and Swan chairs, which have achieved classic status and illustrate Saarinen's dictum that "a chair is a background for the person sitting in it and a piece of sculpture." They swivel to provide privacy and mobility for the user, compose well from every angle, and quietly populate any room.

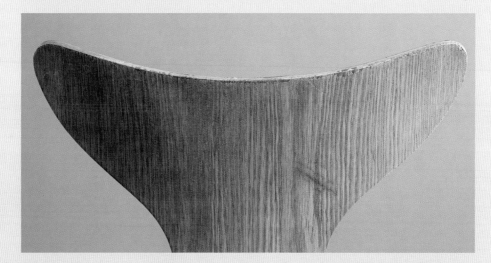

The vital thing is . . . the actual creative activity, whether it's a teaspoon or a national bank. — ARNE JACOBSEN

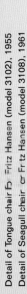

Detail of Tongue chair for Fritz Hansen (model 3102), 1955
Detail of Seagull chair for Fritz Hansen (model 3108), 1961

ARNE JACOBSEN

Clockwise from top left:
Giraffe chair for the SAS Royal Hotel, Copenhagen, 1958
Swan chair for Fritz Hansen (model 3320), 1957/58
Drop chair for SAS Royal Hotel, Copenhagen, 1959
Egg chair for Fritz Hansen (model 3316), 1957/58

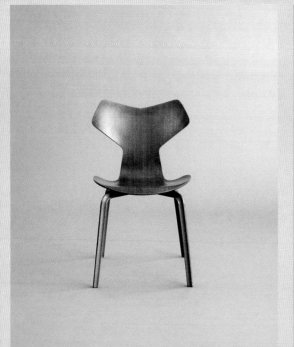

Grand Prix side chair for Fritz Hansen (model 3130), 1957
Armchair for Fritz Hansen (model 3107), 1955
Seagull chair for Fritz Hansen (model 3108), 1961
Tongue chair for Fritz Hansen (model 3102), 1955
Stacking chair for Fritz Hansen (model 3105), 1955
Ant chair for Fritz Hansen (model 3100), 1952

Michael Boyd **CHASING MODERN: IDEAL AND OBJECT**

I've been chasing modern—seeking and hunting, exploring and researching—for twenty-five years now. I'm chasing modern in the sense that I scour flea markets, secondhand shops, auction houses, and collectors' homes, looking for vintage twentieth-century architectural design. When I'm asked where I get the pieces, I reply "anywhere and everywhere." I'm a devoted collector and it is an all-consuming preoccupation.

I'm also chasing modern in the sense that I'm constantly pursuing the elusive and broad definitions of what modern was, as well as what modern is today. This is done in the library and in museums: reading accounts, cross-referencing, and honing my visual memory. I love to situate art and design—to situate the work in history, and to situate the pieces in my home.

Essentially my quest could be called the search for the roots of radical design. Of course this can include traditional African art and ancient Japanese stone sculptures, but here I will concentrate on the beginnings of radical design in Modernism. I am enthralled with the development of the technologies that defined the forefront of modern design: bentwood, tubular steel, vacuum plastics, to name a few. I also have always been fascinated by the way an architect's or designer's universe is present in works of all scales—as Gio Ponti refers to the spectrum of design, "from the spoon to the city." Questions create my agenda as I go on my gathering adventures: What is pioneering modernism with its high ideals and utopian agendas? What is derivative, or kitsch, and falls below the radar? What do I save? What should I reject? Is this important design? Does it contribute to the greater dialog? But mostly I have no specific idea what I'm looking for until I see it. Then I know. I don't know why I know, but I know. Once I track down a piece, there are practical questions: Is it original? Does it need restoration? How do I get it home? There are lofty and transcendent aspects to the chase and real-world problems to be solved.

So the hot pursuit boils down to these two things: There is chasing the modern idea (or ideal/concept) and chasing the modern thing (or object/artwork). The idea I chase in books and at galleries; the object I chase at the markets and auctions. This involves both homework and legwork.

Chasing modern is an absorbing mental and physical exercise that has led to a dedicated philosophy of life. It allows me to be in a constant state of discovery—the discovery of things in unlikely places and the discovery of ideas that enrich our daily lives.

Gio Ponti Detail of occasional table for Pietro Chiesa, c. 1950

The Ideal

My search for the roots of radical design has led me to ask the same questions again and again: What is simple, elemental, and quiet art, architecture, and design, with no cross talk or background noise? I seek spaces and artifacts in which the fundamental nature of the design, abstracted from the dense traffic of choices, has no tricks, gimmicks, irony, or other devices. There must be core content; this was a central stipulation of the minimalist movement. I think, ultimately, it is because of the culture in which I grew up (late twentieth-century America, with its aggressive advertising billboards and deafening film trailers) that I am allergic to hype. I have been brought up to question things and make decisions for myself. I have often joked with my friends that I gravitate toward minimalism so naturally because I can't comprehend anything more. The truth is I am interested in what might be called the "intentionality" of the object. Objects have a morality, or at least they have an obligation in my mind: to be necessary, to be brief, to be useful, to be beautiful, and so on. Of course, when considering art or photography I throw all this out the window—nothing has to make sense at all. But with tools for living, furniture, and design, the nonessential should be eliminated, and all the great functionalist form-givers have followed this path. In a building, a painting, a chair, a book, a graphic design, or a ceramic, the search for simplicity is ironically an advanced one—an acquired taste. The designer begins the exercise with many givens and established baggage that must be dismissed. Manufacturers have mandates; the consumers have expectations. People insist that a fork must be this way, or a chair must perform that way. Many times it is not assuming anything—having a blank slate—that leads to the most ground-breaking and powerful results. It's a funny notion that most minimalist work, in some sense, begins with too much information or complexity and must be reduced: Subtraction is progressive!

I often find that I need the perspective of time to see things clearly. Usually, a generation (twenty to thirty years) seems like a good interval. This is not to say that recent work is automatically weaker. There are certainly some superb designs being created today. But, overall, it seems that evaluating the importance of art and design in the heat of the moment it was created can yield unreliable results. Only after all of the initial marketing propaganda and hearsay has fallen away can one get any sense of whether there's been a real contribution or an emperor's clothes scenario.

In the field of collecting twentieth-century decorative arts, or even modernist houses for that matter, fashions, trends, cycles, and markets, swirl nonstop. Architects, artists, and designers are continuously forgotten or trivialized then rediscovered and idolized by critics, curators, aesthetes, historians, and the consumer. And their markets can be greatly affected. It is precisely these mercurial aspects of collecting that I strenuously try to avoid. I make a policy of acquiring things based on whether or not a museum with similar emphasis would be interested. So, we can conclude that an informed survey of "classic modern" is not really a fixed cannon, but is in perpetual flux. Yet the constant reevaluation can be exhilarating and enlightening, and the chase for quintessential modern design continues.

A good deal of the research and discovery regarding the different meanings of Modernism happens at home in my library. I begin and end every day here. It is the most peaceful and safe place I know. This is the environment where I can try to understand a founding movement's ambitious utopian ideals. I can get the best

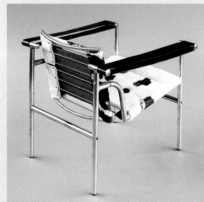

Theo Van Doesburg De Stijl mailer for periodical, c. 1925

Le Corbusier, Charlotte Perriand, and Pierre Jeanneret Basculant armchair for Thonet (Model B301), 1929

insight into an artists' resolute sense of purpose; I can even entertain philosophical debates within the implied morality and ethics of the artworks. Here I am constantly reading and rereading the dogmatic manifestoes of the pioneering architects, artists, and designers.

I admire and respect Adolf Loos's provocative "Ornament and Crime," a polemical [1908] essay that calls for a decisive turn away from applied decoration of any kind and a rejection of outside or primitive influences in favor of concentrated purity. In some ways, for me, that says it all, but from our contemporary perspective, the language comes off as somewhat preachy. And I am deeply moved by the efforts of the Dutch De Stijl movement (Mondrian's paintings, Rietveld's furniture, and J.J.P. Oud's buildings) although much of Theo Van Doesburg's crusading in his "De Stijl" periodical is far too idealistic and oversimplified. Certainly any object must be considered relative to the time of its inception, but the artwork or design must be able to survive its original era and become, for lack of a better description, "timeless" or "universal" modern. It is interesting to note that the artwork is more enduring than the language associated with it. Yet even after the design has passed tough scrutiny, my most ambitious goal has always been to evaluate each piece based on whether or not it resonates in a fresh and contemporary way.

It is fascinating to discover which of the modern movements had a vision of the future and which groups had a dialogue with the past. Which solutions for a design sprang out of technological advancements? Which ones came under the influence of painting or other artistic disciplines? The point is: I do not take the rhetorical justification of the work too seriously. Does the work hold up on its own merit without the verbal or written explanation? Does it stir something in me? It is important to know the original context of a design. What was the cultural climate like when the idea was new?

More than artists' writings, it is in the reading of the objective history that I am most totally absorbed: 1925—Breuer, Mies, and Mart Stam reform bicycle frames into the first tubular steel chairs; 1941—Charles and Ray Eames invent the "Kazam!" machine, and they pioneer the convex bending of plywood, starting a revolution in low-cost furniture. How can a design from 1870 by Christopher Dresser presage a design from 1970 by Joe Colombo? By some definition, everything's been done before: Isn't Le Corbusier's and Charlotte Perriand's Basculant chair really an updated version of a nineteenth-century British campaign chair? The most gratifying aspect of studying the history of modernist ideals is that eventually you arrive at your own. For me the idea is this: I like living in the present, surrounded by things from the past that shaped the future.

Donald Judd has said that if "architecture or design violates its function, it's simply ridiculous." And Immanuel Kant, the eighteenth-century philosopher, argued the other side of the same view. He proclaimed that an object must be useless to be considered art. The implication is that art is the thing you keep around even if it has no purpose. Design must perform, and art must function as an object of contemplation or spiritual transportation. This notion of Judd's and Kant's has become my philosophy in the search for these treasures. It certainly is a basis for our collection: no wordy polemics, no footnotes, and no explanations—just pure form and function in design, and transcendence and inspiration, in art.

Beyond the intellectual underpinnings, there is nothing as immediately potent and visceral as finding the treasure (sometimes among the trash)—a Josef Hoffmann Wiener Werkstätte object at a flea market in Amsterdam or Paris, or a big run of *Arts and Architecture* in a box at the Rose Bowl in Pasadena.

The Object

Although I eventually graduated to auction houses, I began my searches at swap meets and second-hand shops. It can be a chore to sift through all of the discarded junk to maybe find a Verner Panton plastic stacking chair or an Ettore Sottsass Valentine typewriter. I have often thought that I had stumbled upon a highly competent abstract painting only to find out that it is a panel from a broken sewing machine box. And since seeing and contextualizing is what it's all about—this can be fulfilling, too. Some artists would sign the panel as a found object. I'm happy enough leaving it there, with a new perspective in tow. But the real key is keeping my eye on the larger issue. No matter which single objects enter our lives, it is the integrated scheme that is most captivating. Ultimately the goal is to create a total environment, a convincing combination of objects and ideas that reveal the clarity and artistry of high Modernism. I am hunting for things that, when combined, create a rich and unified whole greater than the sum of the individual pieces—a total work of art. The closest word to describe this complete synthesis of art, architecture, and design is the German *Gesamtkunstwerk*.

I'll begin the anecdotes with a real heartbreaker. In 1987 I was driving in the Arizona desert, outside of Phoenix, when I noticed a salvage yard overflowing with modern tables. I immediately recognized the design as Frank Lloyd Wright's from the Arizona Biltmore (1931); there he had collaborated with Warren McArthur and his brother and was responsible for the lobby appointments. This provocative pile of steel was made up of 150 painted steel octagonal tables that were being virtually given away. I thought to myself: "I should get them all." Upon further reflection, I thought, "I should get a bunch, keep one, and sell the rest." I reconsidered again: "At the very least, I should just get one because it's such a great design." Finally, after much deliberation, I came to a decision: "My flight is in an hour, and I don't really know how I'd ship it or deal with it logistically. I won't get any." Well, this line of reasoning turned out to be quite feeble in retrospect. The obvious move would have been to miss my flight and figure it out. I went back to California, saw one example in far lesser condition for the price of a car, and almost fainted. The ones in Arizona had a beautiful Cherokee red paint; the one in town was repainted poorly. Needless to say, when I went back (which was immediately) all of the tables were gone. The most disconcerting part of the ordeal was not the windfall I had just missed out on, but wondering what happened to all of those Frank Lloyd Wright tables. They never showed up on the secondary market. So unless there's a super decked-out bingo hall in Bisbee, Arizona, we all don't know about, I think the tables were melted down as scrap. This is a preservationist's nightmare. While it wasn't on the scale of Neutra's Maslon house, a masterwork recently demolished in Palm Springs, it's a sizable loss. This is exactly the kind of story that lends a sense of urgency to the hunt. I'm more determined than ever to rescue meaningful material. And I'm happy to say

I've learned my lesson—intervene with fate and save the great things while you have a chance.

I acquired our René Herbst 1930 Sandows chair from the greatest imaginable source. Our friends Stephane and Catherine deBeyrie, internationally renowned purveyors of vintage modernism, brought me to Stephane's legendary mother, Maria de Beyrie, in Paris. She was the first Paris dealer to really focus on the Bauhaus stripped-down aesthetic and early French functionalism. She also happened to be a good friend of René Herbst's. Herbst's Sandows design had always been one of my favorite forms and concepts: an elegant tubular steel frame supporting these "objets trouvés"—standard bungee cords made for the industrialized automotive industry. And I considered the possibility of owning such a piece a major addition—it had all the signs of something that would be a defining work in our collection. The bungee cords, which serve as the seat and back, are made of a disposable, low-cost material. I think, more than anything else, I love things like the Sandows chair that are conceptually advanced but may be technically challenged in their final state (as opposed to, say, Poul Kjaerholm's work, which is, in my opinion, technically advanced and conceptually challenged). We own an example of Otto Wagner's stool from the Postal Savings Bank in Vienna. It's a hundred years old, and the bentwood rails' memory is returning. The rails have warped and twisted their way back to where they were headed. The object has a magnificent dualism. On the one hand, it suggests an attempt to be a product of industrial manufacture. Wagner sought the mastery of the built environment: man over nature. At the same time, the tree continues to creep; it is unstoppable and finally cannot be managed. The founding father of rationalism creates a quirky, eccentric, totem fetish.

The Sandows chair has the same magical properties as the Wagner stool. I knew the Sandows example at the Vitra Design Museum had splayed and badly damaged bungee cords, and the versions of Herbst's masterpiece at the Centre Georges Pompidou and MoMA were in a similar state of disrepair. Stephane drove me outside of Paris to a basement storage that was, to my amazement, housing the office of René Herbst intact—his stationery and personal papers, models and drawings, prototypes and rarities were scattered all around. Maria de Beyrie was the executor for the estate and, among other things, had three examples of the Sandows chair. All of the examples were in a patented, blackened, patinated steel and had loose, lost, or splayed bungee cord as usual. However, I immediately did the visual math: There were three chairs, and if all of the perfect bungee cords were consolidated, there could be one perfect example of this phenomenal form. I asked in my comically broken French: "I am a crazy collector, may I make one perfect chair?" Maria replied, "but of course." Now I feel that we may have one of the best examples in the world of this particular design. This is real insight into the mind of a possessed collector. My mother has joked with me, "You're not the Met, you know." Crestfallen on some level, I always respond that, well, you know, one has to try.

Another case of being in the right place at the right time was when we came upon all of the exotic palm trees for the restoration of the Niemeyer house gardens. In fact, one of our reservations in going forward with the purchase of the property was that doing an entire landscape from scratch was just too intimidating and costly. I had filled in plants before on other projects, but I had never created an

entire site. The previous owner was a developer who was going to demolish the house and had already essentially cleared the lot of plants and trees. In some ways it was a lucky turn; the trees that had been removed were quaking aspen and badly pruned spindly pines—not appropriate at all for the true nature of the project. I wanted to infuse the landscape with much more of a sense of the tropical and exotic—I wanted to create the sensation that the Brazilian jungle was closing in.

In a remote part of Southern California, Gabrielle and I were driving by an auto body repair shop, when I couldn't help but notice dozens of different exotic trees—all mature. I turned the car around and Gabrielle asked me where I was going. When I said I wanted to look at the tropical specimens, Gabrielle said that it was an auto body shop and did not appear to be a plant store. I said I had noticed. But how odd that those trees were so old, large, and unusual, even rare, yet they were still in boxes above the ground. Why weren't they in the ground? The planter boxes were weathered and deteriorating; something was up. I found the owner; he said he had a lot-clearing business on the side and couldn't bear to throw these interesting plants away. There were huge palms, bamboos, ferns, and succulents, some of them thirty or forty years old. He said he would sell them, and we agreed on a price. I returned to the car, thrilled, and announced to Gabrielle, "We just got the entire garden in a single stroke!" We had just reached the end of our construction budget. We had decided the week before that we would reconsider the landscaping later, as we could not do it the optimal way at that stage. But now, just a few days later, we had twenty major trees to anchor the entire grounds plan. We were set on doing a convincing Roberto Burle Marx–like landscape throughout the property. A frequent Niemeyer collaborator, Burle Marx brought the vocabulary of forms in modern art to the landscape and his signature hardscapes. There are legendary stories of his plant-collecting expeditions with friends and associates around the lush expanses of his property in Brazil. Clippings were the fruits of the hikes, and often they were replanted next to his house that day. I thought to myself: What a tremendous fast track to the final effect. When I went to pick up the trees and plants I mentioned to the owner, "I've really been having trouble finding oversized rocks," and I showed him the dog-eared Roberto Burle Marx books I was always carrying around with me. He said "Boy, now you should see my giant boulder collection!" We proceeded to a lot across the street, and there was everything necessary to complete the exterior picture: a perfect group of massive stones that could delineate and articulate the entrance to the house—again a concept put forth in a Burle Marx garden design. I made copious sketches, but eventually I just intuitively decorated with enormous trees and rocks in my outdoor room. The crane operator, exasperated with my constantly shifting instructions, thought I was mad for shooting from the hip that way. But it was all installed just as you see it today.

Gabrielle and I were excited when our private obsession bloomed into something of public interest. In 1998 we had an exhibition at SFMOMA entitled *Sitting on the Edge*. The notion was that we were sitting at the precipice—the very threshold of what constituted a chair, a couch, or a clock. Was Nelson's Marshmallow really a sofa? Is Rietveld's Steltman chair really best understood as a super-graphic symbol? Also the exhibition tried to explore the idea that modern design was really microarchitecture

Principles at play with architects' large-scale buildings, and even city-planning grids for that matter, can be seen in, say, the joinery or cantilevering in a piece of furniture. As I mentioned earlier, for the form-givers, the built environment includes every last detail—nothing is inconsequential. Engineering and design is the same in micro form; Josef Hoffmann flatware is easy to recognize if you know his architecture. The vision of Jean Prouvé is evident in everything he touched, from a letter opener to a chair to a commercial building. This nonhierarchal approach was always a central thrust of our collection. Many of the pieces exhibited at SFMOMA were not particularly valuable in monetary terms, but their contribution to the history of modern design was pivotal. I can't help but think of Carlo Mollino's own interior at the Casa Mollino in Torino, Italy. The designer of the world's first four-million-dollar modernist table chose to populate his abode with common, mass-produced, vinyl stools (the Tulip) by Eero Saarinen. They complemented Mollino's own anthropomorphic designs seamlessly. Carlo Mollino, ultimately a surrealist, could not have been more selective. And the overall effect was undeniably powerful—the base of the Tulip stools look like giant pools of milk being poured on the floor.

My search for the essence of modernity, and a dream of the ultimate installation of the collection, eventually took us to Manhattan where we staged a multiyear resurrection of the Paul Rudolph penthouse and apartments on Beekman Place. The Niemeyer house is our seventh restoration of a modernist house; the Rudolph was our fifth. We did our usual due diligence and researched the state of the building and its history. We contacted and retained architects from the Rudolph office who had worked on the project originally. We hunted down scarce plastics to rebuild constructivist cabinets and got oversized plate Plexiglas to repair the floors

Installation views *Sitting on the Edge*, San Francisco Museum of Modern Art, 1998

WALTER AND ELISE HAAS GALLERIES

SITTING ON THE EDGE
MODERNIST DESIGN FROM
THE COLLECTION OF MICHAEL & GABRIELLE BOYD

that were suspended in space. Like a museum conservator, I followed a simple routine: minimal invasiveness—never replace what can be revived—and exhaustive attention to detail. Always, when attempting these architectural overhauls, my main objective is to be invisible. Original blueprints and drawings revealed that what was drawn was very different from what was built. Layer upon layer of surface unfolded before me in a dizzying kaleidoscopic fashion. In fact, the Rudolph penthouse, begun in 1975 and worked on feverishly until the architect's death in 1997, was really a laboratory for experiment, invention, and variation, not a fixed idea revolving around unity. Maybe, in the final analysis, a client's parameters and constraints make for better architecture. This vertigo-inspiring masterpiece was created for Rudolph's own use. Once again, we found ourselves on the edge. But this time we were at a crossroads: What is the minimum requirement for a dwelling? What is the accepted definition of a floor? Do we need doors to make a room? Do we need railings and other conventions? Had we finally become so "edgy" that we actually fell off the edge? It is open to interpretation. And this is, I suspect, the overarching aspect to the collecting and restoring that interests me most: It's all open to interpretation. There is no single vantage point from which to see things; the opposing interpretations of modern art create a rich and dynamic forum. Buildings, like all artworks, can be difficult or challenging. And although the Rudolph laboratory was not a perfect fit as a permanent residence for a family, this difficulty did not detract from its art content.

All of the elements—the study, the treasure hunting, the hands-on rebuilding of modernist architecture, the salvaging of relics, the accumulating of bizarre and disparate objects of art—have one thing in common: constant change and flux. The target is always moving. Just when you think you have a code, or at least a grasp, late-breaking developments—fresh ways of interpreting—suggest a new direction. It is the open road, born out of this new direction, that I want to travel. Sometimes I feel like I have to explore these pieces myself; no reproduction (on paper, or in 3-D) will suffice, whether it's a building or a tea strainer. I have to handle and inspect the original work itself. If I'm chasing down a painting, a piece of modern architecture to restore, or a Bauhaus ashtray, all investigations have led to the same conclusion. I have to learn the real meaning of this loaded, overused, word "modern" firsthand. People ask me: "How do you know that chair is what you think it is?" Occasionally I have no better answer than: "because I have handled a great many of these—turned them upside down and examined them." I'm still trying to memorize the pitch-perfect ratios and proportions of a rough-hewn Schindler chair.

And of course, like all collectors, we periodically have to sell things to make room for the newly found, or to raise funds for the latest project. Water that isn't flowing becomes stagnant. Markets change, new chapters are written, and histories are reinvented, but one thing doesn't change. Good goes with good. Miraculously, it's that simple. Nobody ever bothered to tell me that the permanent design collection on the fourth floor of MoMA was a bad interior scheme—with every imaginable style crashing into the neighboring design. I thought I had never seen anything so beautiful. Oscar Niemeyer himself has said: "It's not a question of ancient or modern. It's a question of good or bad." It's a straightforward issue of quality over style. Good ideas that are well executed will always find their place. Nothing is perfect, but that doesn't mean we should abandon the art of perfecting. I have found

that if you are a curious student of Modernism, open to art content of all kinds, an exciting life lies ahead. You can make educated guesses, cross your fingers, and fill in gaps, but finally, it is the very path of discovery that has the most profound meaning. The process is the total program, and one I would not trade for anything.

Bart Van Der Leck with **Piet Elling** Desk, c. 1925

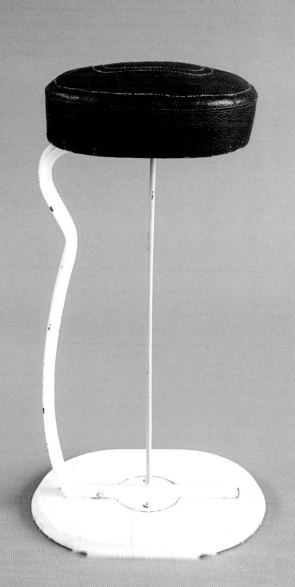

Carlo Mollino Chair for Lisa and Gio Ponti, 1940

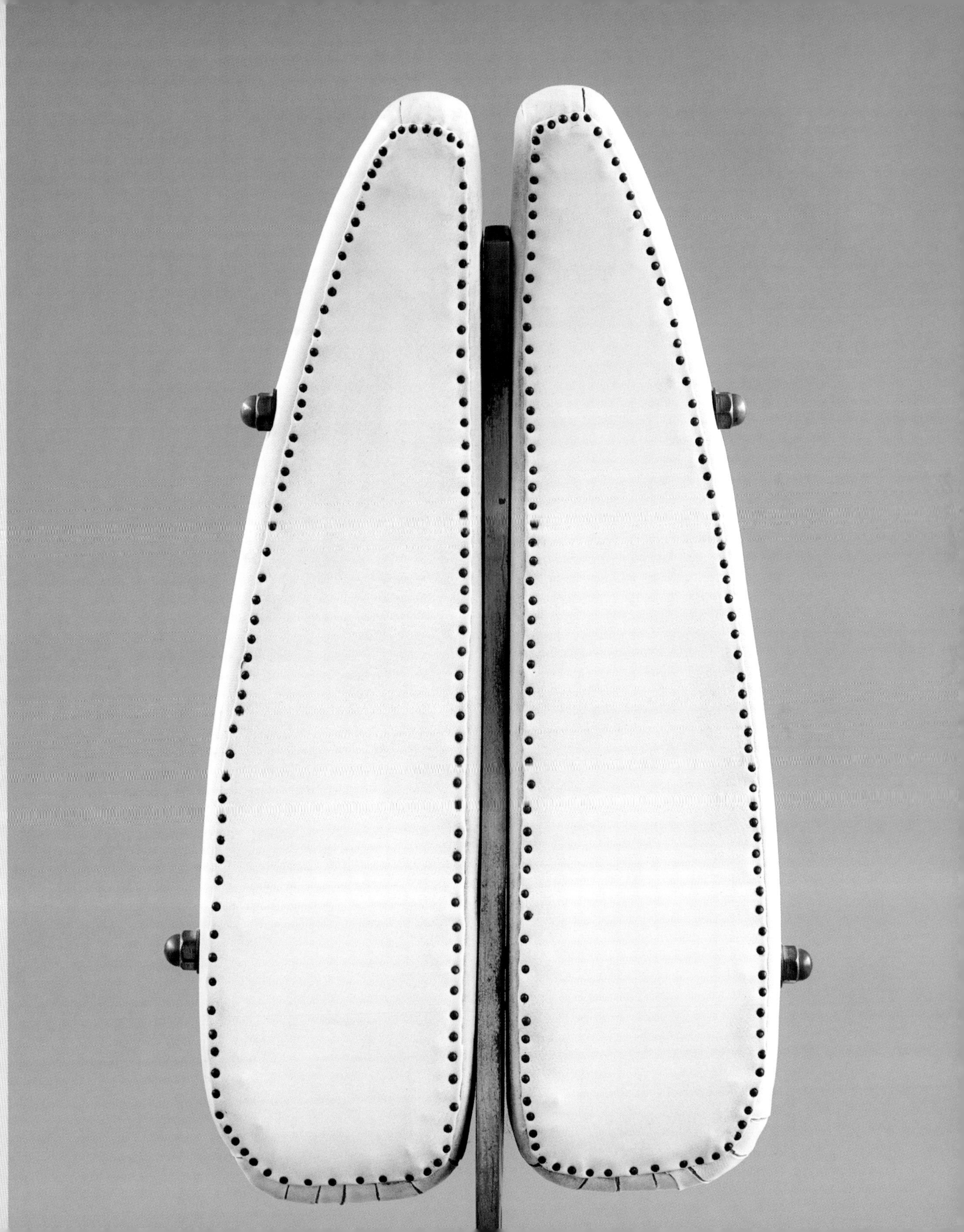

Pierre Chareau Desk, c. 1927

Erich Mendelsohn SS-64 armchair for Desta, 1930

Marcel Breuer Slatted armchair executed at the furniture workshop, Staatliches Bauhaus, Weimar, 1922–24

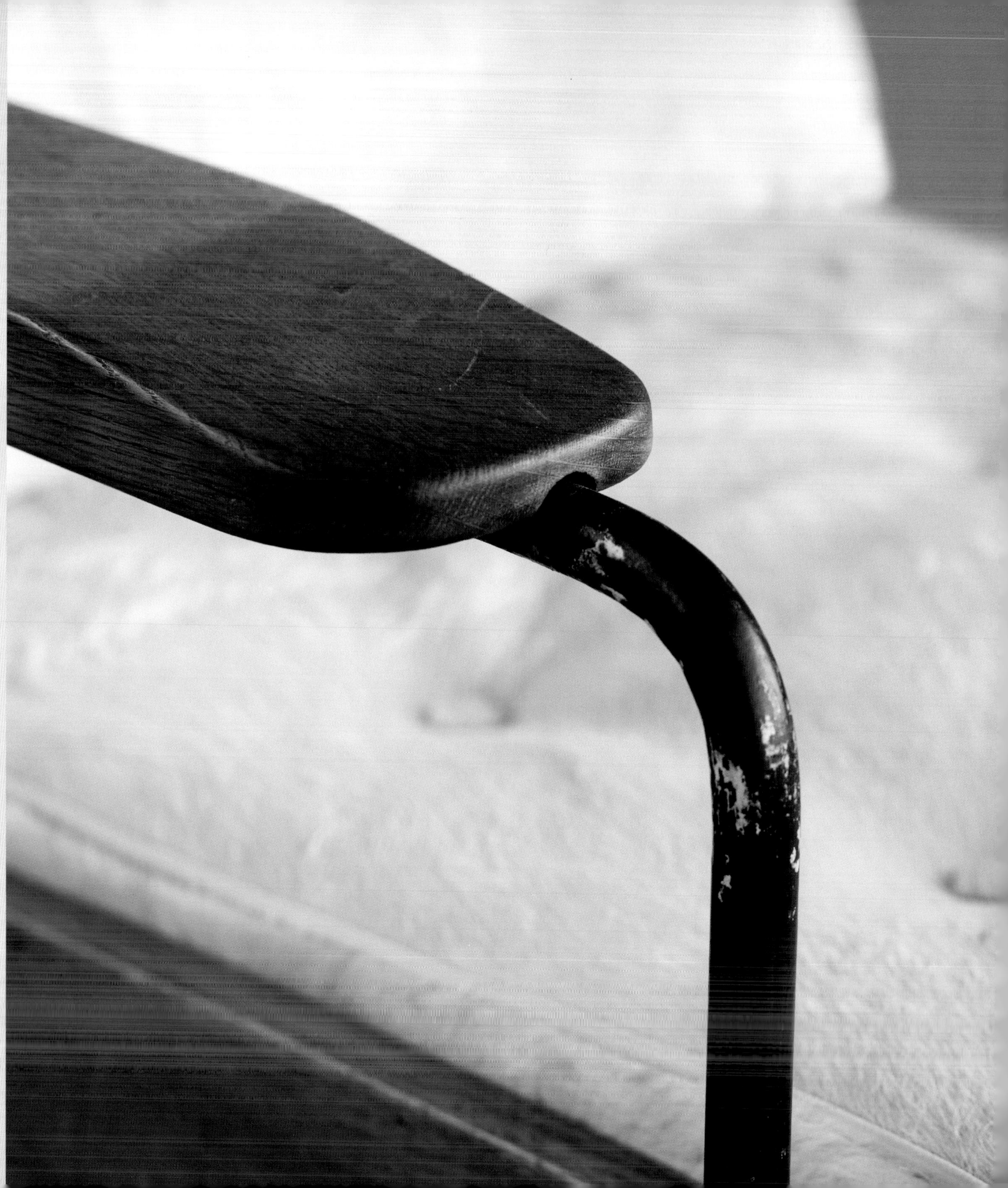

Jean Prouvé Visiteur armchair, 1942

J. J. P. Oud Tubular steel armchair for Metz & Co., 1933/34

Robert Mallet-Stevens Tubular steel lounge chair, c. 1928

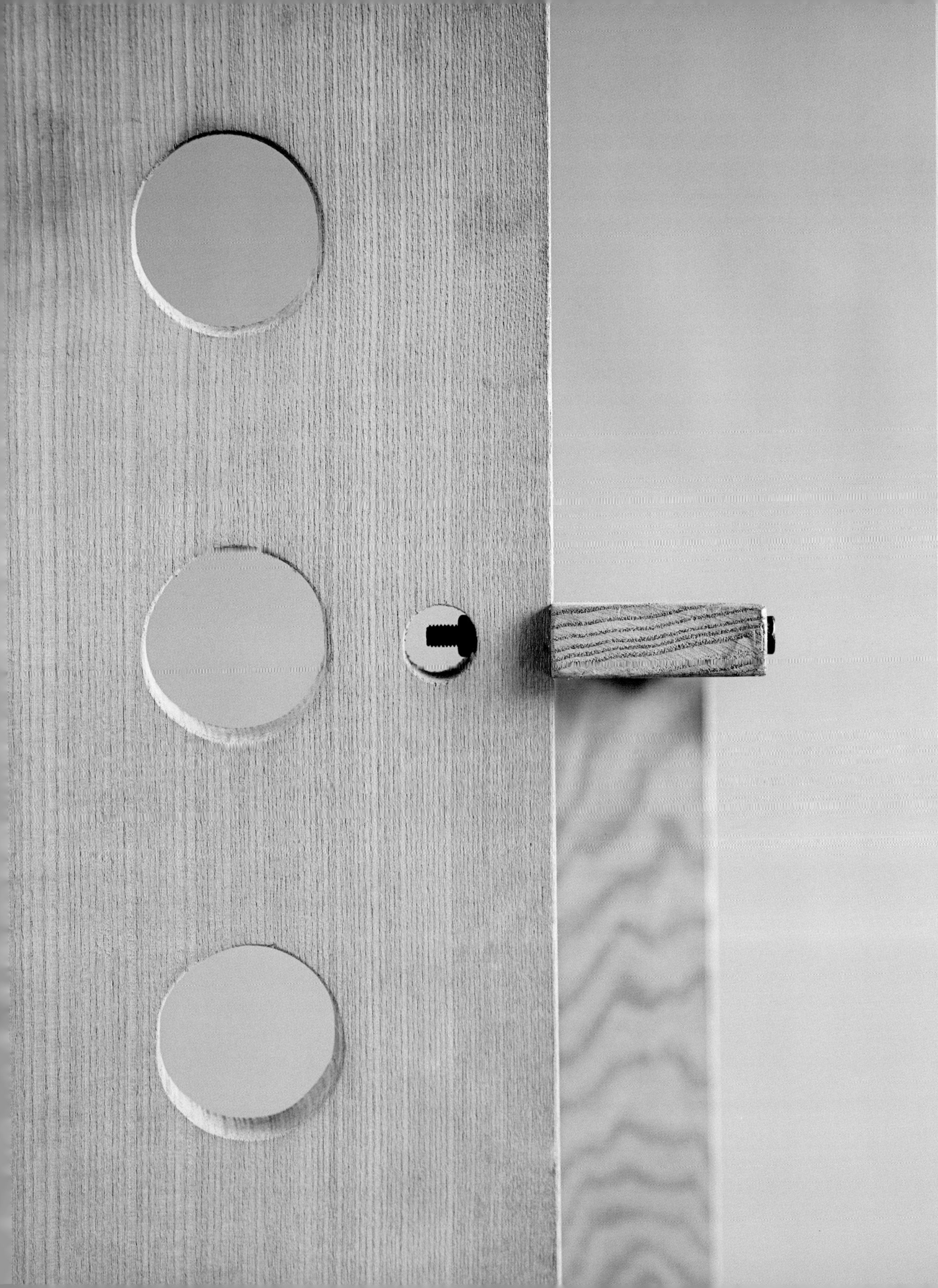

Gerrit Rietveld Moolenbeek Zig-Zag chair, 1942

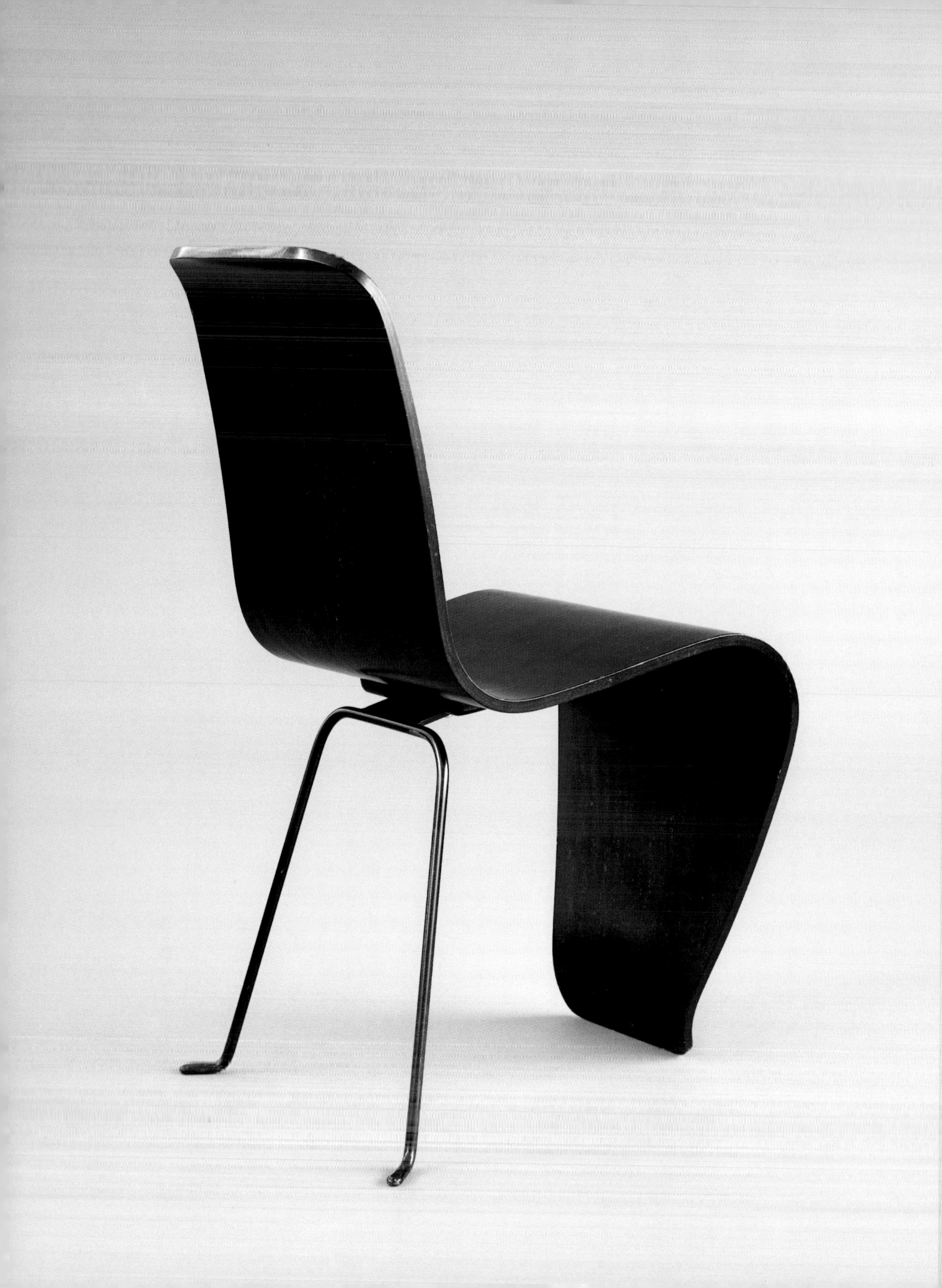

André Bloc Bellvue chair prototype model, 1950

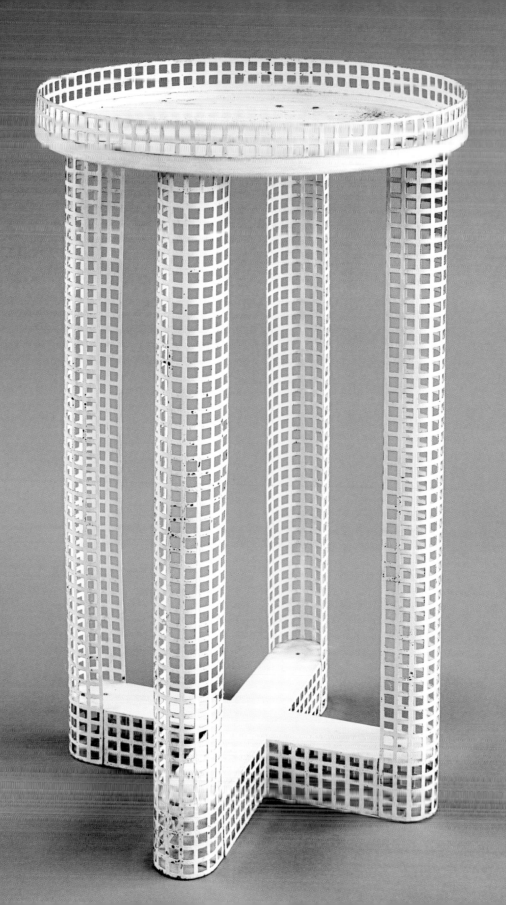

Josef Hoffmann Occasional table for Wiener Werkstätte, 1905

René Herbst Sandows chair, 1928/29

Jean Burkhalter Armchair for Paris Exposition, 1937

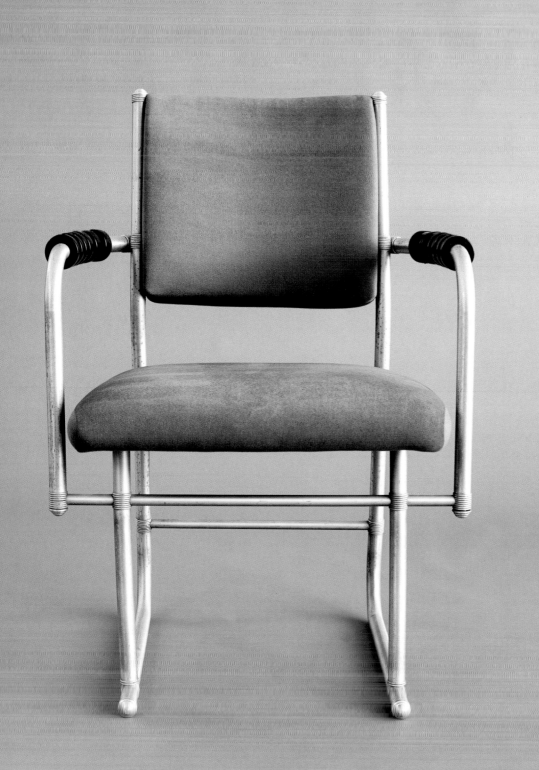

Rudolph Schindler Sardi's restaurant armchair, 1932

Gabrielle Boyd **LIVING MODERN**

While visiting Amsterdam last summer our family hopped into a taxi and asked
the driver to take us to Walem, a restaurant we all love that was designed by the
architect Gerrit Rietveld. Our driver was not a big fan of Rietveld and told us a joke,
"What did Rietveld eat for breakfast?… Not much!" We laughed even though we think
very highly of Rietveld. Our self-appointed guide then proceeded to inform us that the
big problem with Rietveld is that he doesn't believe in fairy tales. We didn't tell him
that we don't believe in fairies either, but that is exactly what we adore about Rietveld
and Judd, and Eames and Prouvé and the other designers who created the objects
that have come to populate our home. They have embraced reality, accepted the world
as it actually is, and attempted to design a better way to live in it. Living modern is
about embracing progress, choosing reality over fancy and honesty over embellishment.

Michael and I were both raised in the sixties in California and
were immediately immersed in counterculture. Our parents were progressives, and dis-
dain for tradition was normal for us. Both of our mothers were creative nest-builders
who adhered to the bohemian style of the hippies—wicker and oak with creeping
houseplants and just basically anything antique. We both acquired from our mothers a
taste for patina, the mellow soulfulness that time grants to objects. Neither of us has
ever lived in a brand-new house with brand-new furniture, yet when we began to fur-
nish our own house, we wanted something fresh. Our first pieces were American
mid-century classics by Eames and Nelson. We continued to explore the possibilities
and expand our horizons by building a library, book by book, to educate ourselves regarding the pioneers of the twentieth-century avant-garde. We followed the trail of the
postwar Europeans working in America back through France, Germany, Austria, and
the Netherlands. We discovered that Charles Eames and Josef Hoffmann were simpa-
tico, as were Jean Prouvé and Peter Behrens. It quickly became clear to us that good
design goes with good design, that good ideas belong together. We rank items on the
basis of quality, not monetary value. We began by furnishing our house and, along the
way, discovered a way of life.

Because we don't believe in fairy tales we understand that if we
want to live in paradise, we need to create it ourselves. Over the years, we have eliminated all bad design from under our roof. It actually is not as difficult as one might
think and is often less expensive. If you know where to look you might just bag an old
original piece for less than a brand-new, cheaply manufactured copy and possibly even

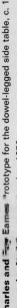

less than a souvenir miniature. By shunning objects with no nutritional value we attempt to avoid becoming swept up by consumerism and overstimulated by ornament. We buy very few brand-new things, and those we buy are mostly limited to new technology. Otherwise we shop at flea markets, antique galleries, and auction houses. Not only is the experience of shopping greatly enhanced, but the impact on our quality of life in the home has been enormous. Once purged of ill-conceived objects, we are free to transcend the clutter and contemplate more interesting propositions. For us it is impossible to think clearly when bounded by bad ideas and, conversely, when surrounded by rational purity one tends to believe in utopia again. The effect of being in the company of nothing but clear ideas is almost meditational.

Seeking enlightenment through the amassing of stuff is surely ironic and possibly only rationalization, however, we have saved many precious objects from both the literal and the figurative trash heaps. These things need to be rescued. Unlike a work of literature, which will most likely be preserved for all time (if it is good), an important building or chair or painting can be destroyed forever out of ignorance. There are many endangered species of design that must be documented and protected. The house we now live in was very nearly bulldozed—the only Oscar Niemeyer house in all of North America, almost demolished! The Paul Rudolph townhouse on Beekman Place has been shrouded in a brick wall by a nasty neighbor. The breathtaking vistas from those multistory windows and the light and shadows that they cast across the rooms are now gone as if they were only a dream. Certainly buildings need to evolve and adapt to their current surroundings in an organic way, but the annihilation of these great pioneering monuments is a cultural tragedy. Progress is achieved by building upon the innovations of each generation. If we destroy the revolutionary advancements of our predecessors, we will doom ourselves to stagnation. Just as the modernists built on the ideas of enlightenment, we must build on the ideas of the twentieth-century avant-garde if we are to make our own contribution to evolution.

Perhaps the most sublime and innovative residence of all is the Rietveld Schroeder house in Utrecht, the Netherlands. It is precisely for its modesty that this home is so exquisite. Mrs. Truus Schroeder, a young widow with three children, commissioned the then furniture maker (with architectural aspirations) Gerrit Rietveld to build her a house in which she could live in a new way that would reflect the progress of her time. She rejected the ostentatious, bourgeois traditions of the other homes on Prins Hendriklaan in favor of a handmade, incredibly efficient sculpture for living. The scale of the house (like many of Rietveld's designs) is diminutive, which creates an intimacy for family living, and the loftlike open floor plan is entirely adaptable into cozy rooms for privacy. It is like a child's box of magic tricks, with invisible doors and shutters that turn into tables, walls that disappear, and sculptures that turn out to be cabinets. Every detail is essential and correct and beautiful. On the wall in the entrance, the exchange wires for the telephone (brand new at the time) are exposed as an art piece. To get by the conservative building codes, the upstairs living quarters were simply called an "attic." This early house was a prototype for modern living. Mrs. Schroder is a hero and a true pioneer for braving the shock of her neighbors and family in order to blaze the trail for a new kind of life—she understood the luxury of subtlety. For encouragement in living adventurously I often look at the house that Mrs. Schroeder built. It still stands as a fragile monument to the ground-breaking vision of Gerrit Rietveld and Truus Schroeder.

There are many other homes in the world that attest to similar ground-breaking ideals, whether designed by a great master or simply a competent unknown. We are lucky to have lived in a few of them. We have restored and lived in several modern houses on the quest to find the right home for our own family—the right balance between art and function. It has been an interesting adventure in adaptability. Each house has its own magic and its own quirks. There are things that I miss about every house that I've lived in, and yet every house has been my favorite at the time that we lived there. We certainly didn't intend to make a life of rescuing endangered houses—it never would have occurred to us—and yet that is how it has unfolded.

We stumbled upon the Oscar Niemeyer Strick house the day after we sold the Paul Rudolph house. We had also just finished restoring a Thornton Ladd house in Santa Barbara, which was beautiful, but ultimately not big enough to accommodate both our children and our library (we chose the children, but missed the books immensely—it was not home without them). Although we had never considered living in Los Angeles, after seeing the Strick house, it was obvious that this needed to be our next home and could very well finally be the Holy Grail we had been seeking. We had gone back and forth between houses that were either too soft or too hard. Yes, we love avant-garde architecture, but we are a family and we need to be able to live in it. Yes, we are a family and we need certain conveniences, but we refuse to completely sacrifice our aesthetics. This house had it all, pure rational yet organic architecture and functional flow, and it was designed by Oscar Niemeyer, the greatest living modern architect. There was also space for both the children and the books. We soon learned that it had been built for a family very much like our own.

Anne Strick, who built and lived in this house for thirty-eight years, is similar to Mrs. Schroeder—unafraid. She built a modernist monument on a street of more traditional finery. She also had three very sophisticated children for whom she provided an environment that offered both social stimulation and the privacy for introspection. The house was built in a T shape, with the public rooms—living, dining, kitchen—at the base of the T in a vast, wide-open scale with walls of glass. The master bedroom lies on one wing of the T top and the kids' rooms and den on the other. I marvel every day at the efficiency of this layout. The scale of the private rooms is very intimate and cozy, while the public hub is a spacious depot for traffic of family and friends. Although Niemeyer never visited the site, the position of the house on the site in relation to the sun is phenomenal. It can feel like some sort of temple, and I imagine that if I paid close enough attention to the shadows falling across the floor they could tell me the day and date and time.

When we acquired the house it was in almost completely original condition, which makes the task of restoration much easier than if it had been remodeled in the interim. If the house has been maintained as it was built, it is simply a matter of replacing the elements that have deteriorated beyond repair. For example, the kitchen cabinets we simply refinished, but the linoleum floors, which were dated and worn, we replaced. We kept the original pink terrazzo tub enclosure and shower in the master bathroom, but replaced the carpeted floors with white terrazzo. We definitely take more liberties with what we consider to be elements of decoration than we would with architectural details. When we restored the Rudolph house, there were a few people who were scandalized that we removed all of the mirrored Mylar that had been glued to the steel beams. The Mylar was buckling and peeling and had to be

175

removed in order to be replaced. Once all of the Mylar had been scraped from the beams (a messy job), we realized that the space was much calmer without the carnival funhouse mirror effect and decided to paint the steel white, as Rudolph himself had specified on other projects. We reasoned that if ever we wanted the mirrors back, we could glue them up at a later date. At any rate, there are choices to be made in the restoration of architecturally important homes and we try to limit the big changes to the cosmetic or surface elements rather than ripping out walls and redefining spaces. Luckily, here at the Strick house the floor plan feels as if we had designed it ourselves to accommodate our own eccentricities.

A common reaction when curators from museums visit our home is "I can't believe you live with this stuff." I have to admit that their concern is not entirely unfounded. Some pieces are fragile and irreplaceable and do belong in a museum. We do not wear white gloves here. There is the possibility for things to be destroyed (although we definitely try to keep that to a minimum). However, our children don't have any rules that we didn't have growing up (no balls in the house, no shoes on the furniture). We do live here; it is a home, not a museum. Each room has its own function, which determines how it will be furnished. The furniture in the children's rooms is virtually indestructible. The furniture in the public rooms has to be sturdy enough to withstand the occasional chair tipper. The more fragile items are kept in the library, which is off-limits to chair tippers and children unaccompanied by an adult. All of these things were designed to be lived with. Each has a purpose, and that purpose should be manifested in its use. In the end, a house must function as a home, and one should feel not only sheltered, but also nurtured by it.

A house is not just something to live in and a chair is not just something to sit in. By taking the time to make thoughtful choices about our environment, we can add meaning to our lives. We must define the space in which we live or risk being defined by it. The private home is one of the few places where an individual is able to exercise complete authority over his or her environment to achieve not only a personal creative vision, but possibly a Shangri-la. There is no substitution for living among good ideas. For us, there is no turning back. Living in light-filled, open spaces with clean lines and well-reasoned details, filled with only good ideas, is modern, and it is freeing. For thousands of years now, humans have built the most elaborate of nests, generally with display of wealth and homage to the past as the prime motivators. However, the heavy burdens of the past can slow our progress. The modernists contended that romanticism, superstition, and sentimentality were old-fashioned and outmoded. They revolted by re-creating their own world based on reason and the technological advancements of their time. We honor the fearlessness and originality of the modernists in the hope that we too can be fearless and original.

Bedroom Corridor (left to right):
Zulu staffs
Masai sword
Amazon paddles
Indonesian Acehnese
Solomon Islands lance
Samoan paddle

Dressing room:

Nassos Daphnis *Untitled*, oil on board, 1959
George Nelson Miniature chest for Herman Miller (Model 5511), 1955
Stig Lindberg Veckla vase for Gustavsberg, 1950s

(Left to Right):

Charles and Ray Eames ESU 220-N for Herman Miller, 1950

Isamu Noguchi Rocking stool for Knoll, 1954

Stig Lindberg Pungo vases for Gustavsberg, 1950s

Gilbert Watrous Table lamp for Heifitz, c.1950

Tapio Wirkaala Glass Leaf dish for Iittala, 1954

Master Bath:

Gyorgi Kepes Light Abstraction, photograph, c.1939/40

Warren McArthur Table for the Arizona Biltmore Hotel, 1931

Eero Saarinen Tulip stool for Knoll, 1956

Architectural pottery vessels, 1950s

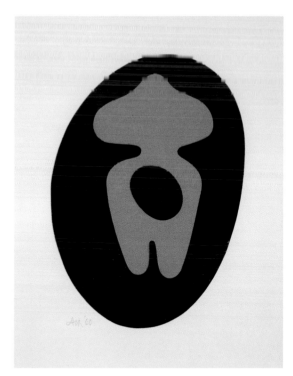

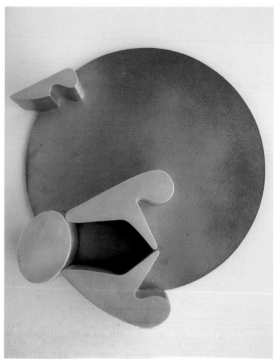

Clockwise from top left:

Sidney Geist *Untitled*, Painted wood relief, 1939

Man Ray *Le Torse Tournant*, bronze sculpture, 1959

Jean Arp *Untitled*, Collage, 1960

André Mounier *Untitled*, Aluminum and bronze relief, 1960

Carlo Scarpa Glass vase for Venini, 1936

Jean Arp *Heads or Tails*, bronze sculpture, 1959

James Prestini *Untitled*, Marble sculpture, 1953

Verner Panton Plastic stacking chair for Herman Miller, 1959/68
Arne Jacobsen Side chair for Fritz Hansen (model 3107), 1955
George Nelson Case goods from the steel frame series for Herman Miller, 1950s

Media Room (et c 1 0):

Ray Eames Time/Lif stools for Herman Miller, 1960

Isamu Noguchi G ss coffee table for Herman Miller (Model IN-50), 1946

Hans Wegner Flag halyard lounge chair (Model GE 225), 1950

Arredoluce F oor lamp 1955

Isamu Noguchi Si e able for Knoll (Model 87), 1956

Paul Rudolph Sof for the Rudolph townhouse. New York, c. 1975

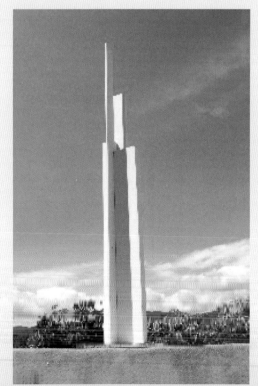

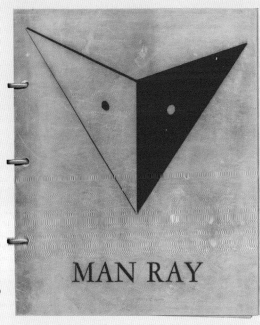

MAN RAY

Otto Lindig ... tea service, c. 1928, produced by Majolika-Manufaktur Karslruhe, various dimensions

ACKNOWLEDGEMENTS

I would like to thank Michael and Gabrielle Boyd for their passion, warm hospitality and unremitting dedication to making this book a worthy celebration of the work of art they have created. At Rizzoli, Charles Miers gave the project his enthusiastic support, and, as editor, Dung Ngo saw it through to publication with unflagging patience and skill. In their images, Tim Street-Porter captured the spirit of the house and Steve Freihon illuminated the beauty of the collection. Lorraine Wild and her associates at Green Dragon deftly wove the strands together.

— M.W.

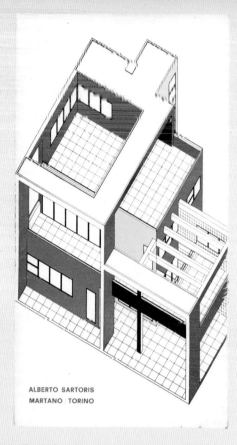

ALBERTO SARTORIS
MARTANO TORINO

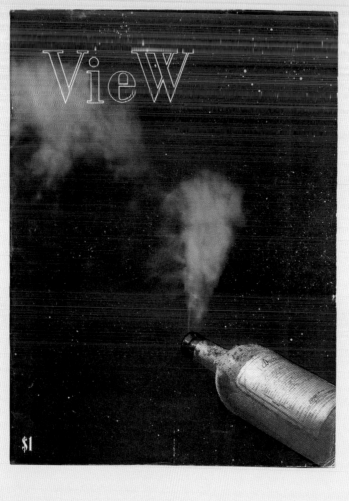

$1

Marcel Duchamp *View, The Modern Magazine*, Marcel Duchamp, Series V, No. 1, New York, 1945, 12" x 9"

Back cover:

Villas Modernes, Roger Roula n, c. 1930

Alexandre Noll Sycamore bowl, c. 1950

Josef Hoffmann with Oswald Haerdtl, Café Chair, 1929

Marcel Duchamp *View, The Modern Magazine*, 1945

Eileen Gray Stool Ponte 1027, 1931-32

Carlo Molline Chair for Lisa and Gio Ponti, 1940

Bart Van Der Leck with **Piet Elling**, desk, c. 1925

Kasimir Malevich *De Gegenstandslose Welt*, 1927

Gerrit Rietveld Hoge stoel dining room chair, 1919

Jean Arp *Untitled collage*, 1960

Fredrick Kiesler, *Contemporary Art Applied to the Store and its Display*, 1930

Isamu Noguchi Model IN-22 Fin stool, 1949

Marcel Breuer Wassily club chair, 1925

Arne Jacobsen Drop Chair for SAS Royal Copenhagen Hotel, 1959

Marcel Breuer Basket drawer unit, c. 1930

Georges Jouve, Glazed ceramic vase, c. 1950

Alexander Rodchenko with V. Stepanova, *Soviet Cinema*, 1935

Jean Prouvé Bar stool, c. 1950

Josef Hoffman vase with glass liner, c. 1905

Josef Muller-Brockmann *Protegette il Bambini* poster, 1953

First published in the United States
of America in 2007 by
Rizzoli International Publications, Inc.
300 Park Avenue South
New York, NY 10010
www.rizzoliusa.com

ISBN-10: 0-8478-2837-9
ISBN-13: 978-0-8478-2837-1
LCCN: 2006933066

© 2007 Rizzoli International Publications, Inc.
"Visionary Design for Living" and
"Modernist Paradise" © Michael Webb
"Chasing Modern: Ideal and Object"
© Michael Boyd
"Living Modern" © Gabrielle Boyd

Designed by Lorraine Wild with Victoria Lam
and Robert Ruehlman/Green Dragon Office

Printed and bound in China
2007 2008 2009 2010 2011 / 10 9 8 7 6 5 4 3 2 1